beyond the VELVET UNDERGROUND

dave thompson

Omnibus Press
London/New York/Sydney/Cologne

© Copyright 1989 Omnibus Press
(A Division of Book Sales Limited)

Edited by Chris Charlesworth
Art Direction by Mike Bell
Book Designed by Ranch Associates
Picture Research by Debbie Dorman & David Thompson
Project and typesetting co-ordinated by Caroline Watson

ISBN 0.7119.1691.8 Order No. OP45087

Exclusive distributors:

Book Sales Limited
8/9 Frith Street,
London W1V 5TZ, UK.

Music Sales Corporation
24 East 22nd Street,
New York, NY 10010, USA.

Music Sales Pty Limited
120 Rothschild Avenue,
Rosebery, NSW 2018, Australia.

To the Music Trade only:
Music Sales Limited
8/9 Frith Street,
London W1V 5TZ, UK.

Picture credits:
EMI Records: p65
Mick Gold: p4, 10, 16, 23(B), 36, 50(T), 52, 76, 88
London Features Int.: p18, 21, 28, 29(T), 32, 34, 40, 48, 50(B), 57, 58, 61(T), 68, 70,
78, 80(T), 81, 84, 90(T&B), 91
Pictorial Press: p6/7, 26, 29(B), 31, 39, 43, 45, 53, 59, 92
RCA: p23(T), 41, 60, 63, 66, 73, 74, 75
Ebet Roberts: p64
Kate Simon: p61(B), 80(B)

Every effort has been made to trace the copyright holders of the photographs in this
book but one or two were unreachable. We would be grateful if the photographers
concerned would contact us.

Typeset by Capital Setters, London.
Printed in England by Anchor Press Ltd., Tiptree, Essex.

1 MASTERS OF MENACE

2 COCKLESHELL AND SURE

INTRODUCTION

Put in the starkest terms, The Velvet Underground was the most influential band to come out of rock 'n' rollin' white America – ever. Elvis Presley might have started the ball rolling in the first place, but it was his hips and that sneer which did it really, and by the time he knew what was going on, he was already on his way to Colonel Tom's reprocessing plant.

Bob Dylan had a suck on the cigar as well, but four classic albums in a quarter of a century, (You want names? Play 'em all and find out for yourself) and a handful of folkie classics doesn't cut any ice this neck of the woods . . . does it, Mr Jones?

So who's left? The Grateful Dead? Bruce Springsteen? James Taylor? Chips off the same block, every man-jack of them. You couldn't call them rock 'n' roll anyway – you couldn't call The Velvets rock 'n' roll either, come to that, but take a snap poll of every band who's meant anything to anyone, from The Stooges on down, and you can bet your life they cut their teeth working out 'Sweet Jane', graduated on to 'Waiting For The Man' and probably go to sleep at nights dreaming of 'Sister Ray'. And who else burned so briefly, but has blazed for so long? The band themselves were long, long gone before most folk even realised what they'd really been doing, latching on to Lou Reed's subliminal brainwash barnstormers, a clutch of neatly packaged MGM compilations, and the name-dropping idolatry which has been going on for 15 years now, and will still be going 15 years from now. It's a convoluted road from David Bowie to The Mary Chain, but wherever there's feedback, The Velvets will be lurking.

But The Velvets deserve better than that. They weren't simply noise merchants; 'Sunday Morning' sounds like The Monkees, 'Who Loves The Sun' sounds crasser than that. Take out 'The Murder Mystery' and Linda Ronstadt could cover the third album. The secret wasn't in the songs, wasn't in the sound. It was the very essence of The Velvets, the existence of The Velvets. *The Tale Of Willy's Rats* came close, at least in as much as it created a microcosm of living legend around a pop group, whether they sprung from Mick Farren's imagination or not. Guy Peelaert's *Rock Dreams* has the same effect. A bunch of pretty pictures? Sure! But scrape away the paint, look under the gaudy repainting of time-trodden imagery and study the heart of the beast. The Velvet Underground was more than a pop group, more than a lifestyle, it was a life in itself. The names changed, the music changed, but for three years, four albums, a few hundred gigs and a tabloid's-worth of sleazoid debauchery stories, The Velvet Underground picked up everything you ever wanted to know about rock 'n' roll and shoved it in your face. With feeling.

The Velvet Underground story has been written and rewritten. Their lives, their loves, their lunches, lovingly recorded and served up hot and cold, ready to bring the next generation of acolytes racing for the altar. This is *not* their story, it is simply their words, their friends' words, and the words of a whole bunch of people who might not even have been alive when The Velvets were kicking. What was so special about The Velvet Underground? It's a personal thing. Read the words, play the tunes, and work it out for yourself. If nothing else, it'll change the way *you* listen to music.

MAST
OF
MENA

ERS

CE

NEW YORK

Where else could I go? I figured if I could make it in New York I could make it anywhere.
JOHN CALE, AUGUST 1975

You never get to play tennis in New York. I wanted to be married in my tennis clothes with a visor and balls all over me and two rackets across the front.
JOHN CALE, 1971

I love it. In New York I can pick up a phone and have anything I want delivered to the door. I can step a foot out into the street and get into a fight immediately. All the energy, people going crazy, guys with no legs on roller skates. It's very intense. The energy level is incredible. It's nice at five in the morning to be stoned on THC and go down to Hong Fows, have some watercress soup, then you take a taxi uptown with some maniac and say, 'Go ahead, drive faster wise guy', and you just zip around. When you go up Park Avenue there's a very funny turn and it's always fun to wonder if they'll make it.
LOU REED, MAY 1973

Living in New York you're not so much worried about eating as you are about people coming up to you for no reason at all and smashing you over the head or sticking you with a knife.
JOHN CALE, FEBRUARY 1983

It makes me uncomfortable and I'm used to it . . . It used to be exciting with always something to pay attention to, but I've been there too long and moving around is no answer to it. But it's slowly sinking in that Wales is no longer my home territory, and that makes me uncomfortable.
JOHN CALE, FEBRUARY 1983

PROTOTYPES

Lou and I actually met in the Creative Writing class which Delmore Schwarz was teaching.
STERLING MORRISON, APRIL 1981

I originally met Lou Reed at a party. I came in with a friend – we both had long hair and some guy approached us and told us we looked very commercial and would we like to meet this band called The Primitives who had this terrible single out, called 'Do The Ostrich'. Lou was in the band, but he was bitter because they wouldn't let him do 'Heroin'.
JOHN CALE, APRIL 1974

I met Sterling on the subway. I hadn't seen him in three years and he didn't have any shoes on and I had boots on and we took him home.
LOU REED, 1983

Sterling had gone to Syracuse with Lou and Mo lived down the road from him. She was a button operator . . . or something by day and in the evening she would go home and play the drums. We had so much trouble with drummers but Mo was good at being basic so she was brought in. Actually Lou was always saying, 'Sterling can't play guitar, and Mo can't play.' He kept saying,

'But man, she can't play.' My idea was to keep the sound simple, but by overlaying the instruments' simplistic patterns the accumulative effect of the sound would be incredibly powerful. I was highly intrigued by the whole Phil Spector Wall-Of-Sound concept but obviously I had to modify it for a four-piece.
JOHN CALE, APRIL 1974

We really didn't have any money, and we used to eat oatmeal all day and all night and give blood and pose for these nickel or 15c tabloids they have every week. And when I posed for them, my picture came out and it said I was a sex maniac killer that had killed 14 children and tape recorded it and played it in a barn in Kansas at midnight. And when John's picture came out in the paper it said he had killed his lover because his lover was going to marry his sister and he didn't want his sister to marry a fag.
LOU REED, SEPTEMBER 1966

We tried to play clubs in Harlem but they wouldn't let us in, we played Larry's Love Nest, we played on the sidewalks. We made more money on the sidewalks than anywhere else.
JOHN CALE, OCTOBER 1974

In 1965 the pop music scene was going to go without us. John had no pop involvement whatsoever, and Lou and I had given up. It was impossible. The bands all had matching suits and dance routines, it was a very cosmetic time. So we said, well, we don't have matching suits and it's very unlikely we'll be able to work out these dance routines, so I guess we've had it. So, Lou, John and I, having concluded that we'd had it, were free to pursue anything we wanted.
STERLING MORRISON, SEPTEMBER 1985

STERLING MORRISON

He's teaching English somewhere, wishing he was in a rock 'n' roll band. When he was in a rock 'n' roll band he wanted to be teaching English.
LOU REED, JANUARY 1976

MAUREEN TUCKER

She's absolutely straight – you keep on looking for the Buster Brown shoes! If something embarrasses her she just turns red!
INGRID SUPERSTAR, SEPTEMBER 1966

You know what her favourite expression is? You piece of shit.
LOU REED, SEPTEMBER 1966

She always said there was no reasoning with any one of us, that we were all crazy, and there was no sense in arguing. I think basically the band had three uncontrollable personalities, and if you throw drugs into the confusion then you really have problems.
STERLING MORRISON, APRIL 1981

I've always been a tomboy so it wasn't strange being one of the first women to play in a rock band. We always played pool together, drank a lot of beer together. But I'm glad to see so many girls playing guitar now.
MO TUCKER, MAY 1981

I always wanted to play drums. You know when you're in the fourth grade and they sign you up for music lessons? Well, I picked drums, but I never went. Then rock 'n' roll came around and I really wanted to get in on the creative end of that. I played guitar for a while, then tambourine, but that wasn't making it, so I got a really cheap drum set.
MO TUCKER, 1983

We needed an amplifier and she had one, plus she's an out of sight drummer. She worked as a computer key puncher and when she'd come home at five she'd put on Bo Diddley records and play every night from five to 12, so we figured she'd be the perfect drummer and she was.
LOU REED, 1983

How Welsh can you get? John Cale's dad was a coal miner.
GIOVANNI DADOMO, *SOUNDS*, JUNE 1977

I don't mind talking about the past. How far do you want to go back? The Napoleonic Wars? I was
scenic adviser at Waterloo.
JOHN CALE, NOVEMBER 1977

Just when you think you've got John Cale figured out, when you think you've got him taped and
you've sussed out what his music is about – well that's the point when all your expectations are
thrown for a loop.
ISLAND RECORDS BIOG, 1974

John Cale. Good Grief I couldn't begin to describe him, he's just funny looking . . . That bohemian
Buffy St Marie look. All he needs is a pair of antennae, then he could be an equivalent to a Martian.
INGRID SUPERSTAR, SEPTEMBER 1966

He looks very Mephistophelian.
LOU REED, SEPTEMBER 1966

John Cale looked like an enormous predatory moth.
ADAM SWEETING, *MELODY MAKER*, FEBRUARY 1984

I really enjoyed school. I'd go in at 8 o'clock and stay as long as I could.
JOHN CALE, JUNE 1977

My parents couldn't afford a guitar and I wasn't really interested in playing and no one seemed interested in forming bands. I used to grease my hair and wear thin ties and be a Teddy Boy. In Wales, man, I used to drive them mad. Be a Teddy Boy and go to the Arts Club. But I wasn't that good at classical music. I failed all my exams. I got to college in London by talking about philosophy more than anything else, saying that I had read H. Stuart Hughes, Bertrand Russell and a bunch of other things. It was all publicity.
JOHN CALE, AUGUST 1975

It was a despairing situation trying to figure out how to be a composer, my mother saying, 'You've got to be a doctor or a lawyer because you'll never make a living as a musician', and then getting to New York I finally got a chance to live out my fantasies with a rock 'n' roll band.
JOHN CALE, FEBRUARY 1983

I learned to play viola at school. It was an allocation orchestra, they had clarinets and flutes and stuff. Everyone else got the clarinets and flutes, all I got was the viola.
JOHN CALE, OCTOBER 1974

When I got to Tanglewood the master class in composition was conducted by Yannis Xenakis, who is a draftsman by training. He worked on the Paris Pavilion. And he had two pieces of music. One was based on a probability theory and consisted of plotting the probability of a B Flat occurring in the next three bars. The other, called 'Metastasis' was based on the plans for the Paris Pavilion and the angles of the building were used as a slide of the glissando. Which is a load of codswallop.
JOHN CALE, APRIL 1981

They would never let me perform my pieces at Tanglewood because they were so violent. Eventually they did let me. I didn't tell them what I was going to do. There was a table and another pianist, I was working away inside the piano and I just took an axe and . . . right in the middle of the table. People were running out of there, but I also had the acolytes who came backstage afterwards in tears. I got all the reactions. It was the element of surprise and I hope I've kept that. It's very important for me to be able to keep leading people up the garden path and then turn around, BOING!
JOHN CALE, SEPTEMBER 1985

By the time I got to New York I felt I'd run my course as far as avant-garde music was concerned.
JOHN CALE, JUNE 1977

Did you know my father was a member of the SS?
JOHN CALE, MAY 1985

John was always exciting to work with. If you listen to his bass part on 'Waiting For The Man', it's illogical, inverted almost. He had really good ideas on bass.
STERLING MORRISON, APRIL 1981

I went to school and I'm not illiterate, which isn't to say that people who go to school are literate. But, for my part, I studied literature, art, drama, movies and even journalism, believe it or not.
LOU REED, APRIL 1983

I was introduced to drugs by a mashed-in faced Negro whose features were in two sections (like a split-level house) named Jaw. Jaw gave me hepatitis immediately, which is pathetic and laughable at once, considering I wrote a famous amplified version of the experience as a song.
LOU REED, *FALLEN KNIGHTS AND FALLEN LADIES*, 1973
(Contribution by Reed to *No One Waved Goodbye* – Charisma Books, 1973, Ed: Robert Somma.)

Who can you talk to on the road? Long-haired dirty drug people wherever you look. The boy passes over a bag of green powder and passes out. Don't take that, it has horse tranquilliser in it. Oh, I shot up to your song, I got busted to your song, oh please bless me and touch me and make it all go away. I loved you.
LOU REED, *FALLEN KNIGHTS AND FALLEN LADIES*, 1973

I take drugs just because in the 20th century in a technological age, living in the city there are certain drugs you have to take just to keep yourself normal like a caveman. Just to bring yourself up and down, but to attain equilibrium you need to take certain drugs. They don't getcha high, even, they just getcha normal.
LOU REED, JULY 1973

Lou Reed looks like a pretty little girl, with short hair . . . He's got brown curly hair, he usually wears sunglasses. And he's slightly built and he's got a pug nose.
INGRID SUPERSTAR, SEPTEMBER 1966

Best of luck to the dead worms.
LOU REED, FEBRUARY 1979

There's a great deal of normalcy about Lou Reed.
DOUG YULE, FEBRUARY 1979

I think he might start writing some good songs again were he to go back and live with his parents. That's where all his best work came from. His mother was some sort of ex-beauty queen and I think his father was a wealthy accountant. Anyway, they put him a hospital where he received shock treatment as a kid. Apparently he was at Syracuse and was given this compulsory choice to either do gym or ROTC (the Reserves Officers Training Corps). He claimed he couldn't do gym because he'd break his neck and when he did ROTC he threatened to kill the instructor. Then he put his fist through a window or something, and so he was put in a mental hospital. I don't know the full story. Every time Lou told me about it he'd change it slightly.
JOHN CALE, APRIL 1974

My liver kept me from the Army.
LOU REED, 1974

Lou's parents hated the fact Lou was making music and hanging around with undesirables. I was always afraid of Lou's parents – the only dealings I'd had with them was that there was this constant threat of them seizing Lou and having him thrown in the nut-house. That was always over our heads. Every time Lou got hepatitis his parents were waiting to seize him and lock him up.
STERLING MORRISON, APRIL 1981

I don't see my parents. We've little to say to each other. They're very middle class. My father owns a very big company. I was supposed to inherit all that. But I didn't. I went out and did the most horrifying thing possible in those days, I joined a rock band. And of course I represent something very alien to them.
LOU REED, JUNE 1977

Reed has the ability to make most interviewers feel uncomfortable in his presence. He has a fixed sinister glare and never smiles. For the most part his speech is very abrupt and evasive.
JERRY GARVIN, MAY 1973

DELMORE SCHWARZ

Delmore was a brilliant poet, but he had a clinical case of paranoia. He thought he was being persecuted by Nelson Rockefeller, and eventually he decided that Lou and I were both Rockefeller's spies.
STERLING MORRISON, APRIL 1981

Delmore Schwarz was the unhappiest man I ever met in my life – and the smartest . . . till I met Andy Warhol. He didn't use curse words till age 30. His mother wouldn't allow him. His worst fears were realised when he died and they put him in a plot next to her.
LOU REED, MAY 1978

No one knows why 'European Son' was dedicated to Delmore. Everyone thinks it's because the song is thematically appropriate – 'You killed your European son, you spit on those under 21.' Incidentally, that may be true because Delmore was the son of Jewish émigrées and a great poet who was never accepted. But the real reason is that it only has two stanzas of lyrics and a long instrumental break. Delmore thought rock 'n' roll lyrics were the worst things he'd ever heard in his life; he despised songs with words. As this was our big instrumental outing on the album we dedicated it to him.
STERLING MORRISON, APRIL 1981

I'm just delighted I got to know him. It would have been tragic not to have met him.
LOU REED, MAY 1978

THE VELVET UNDERGROUND – THE BOOK

There were whips and chains on the cover but it was basically about wife swapping in Suburbia.
STERLING MORRISON, APRIL 1981

THE VELVET UNDERGROUND – THE GROUP (I)

Being in a rock 'n' roll band was my fantasy that I couldn't live out in Wales. It was important that it was different, that's why we had the viola in there. I was glad that Lou had that lyrical ability, but I didn't like his folk songs. I hated Joan Baez and Dylan, every song was a fucking question! But Lou had these songs where there was an element of character assassination going on. He had strong identification with the characters he was portraying. It was method acting in song. The melodies weren't great, so we put arrangements around them, trying to get that grandiose Phil Spector feeling.
JOHN CALE, FEBRUARY 1983

Nico at The Paris Bataclan.

If you look back at the early Velvet Underground, in retrospect it's remarkable. If you look at other areas, there's nothing. The Velvet Underground is legitimate. It can hold its own. I mean, I didn't write *Death Of A Salesman*, but then, I didn't find that an interesting play anyway.
LOU REED, MAY 1978

The first time we played as The Velvet Underground (Summit High School, 11 November 1965) we opened with 'There She Goes Again', then played 'Venus In Furs' and ended with 'Heroin'. The murmur of surprise that greeted our appearance as the curtain went up increased to a roar of disbelief once we started to play 'Venus' and swelled to a mighty howl of outrage and bewilderment by the end of 'Heroin'.
STERLING MORRISON, 1983

Screeching rock 'n' roll – reminded viewers of nothing so much as Berlin in the decadent thirties.
LOS ANGELES MAGAZINE, 1966

One night at the Café Bizarre we played 'The Black Angel's Death Song' and the owner came up and said, 'If you play that song one more time, you're fired.' So we started the next set with it, the all-time version, and got fired.
STERLING MORRISON, APRIL 1981

Our attitude to the West Coast was one of hate and derision. They were into being flower children and beautiful and all that – they were pansying around. It was like some kind of airy-fairy puritanism that was based on the suppression of adult feelings about what was out there in the world. They were being evangelistic about it but they didn't really care. As far as we were concerned, we were just getting on with it.
JOHN CALE, MAY 1975

A three ring psychosis that assaults the senses with the sights and sounds of the total environment syndrome . . . Discordant music, throbbing cadences, pulsating tempo.
VARIETY, 1966

The Velvets were ahead of everybody. It's the only thing that ever, ever, ever swept me off my feet as music since early Mahler. They were a revolution.
DANNY FIELDS, 1983

We never did anything to ingratiate ourselves with the media. Through lack of interest more than arrogance. I was convinced that if it was going to happen it would happen anyway. We were all really contemptuous of hype.
STERLING MORRISON, APRIL 1981

In the beginning, Lou and I had an almost religious fervour about what we were doing – like trying to figure ways to integrate some of (LaMonte) Young's or Andy Warhol's concepts into rock 'n' roll. But after the first record we lost our patience and diligence. We couldn't even remember what our precepts were.
JOHN CALE, AUGUST 1980

The sound is a savage series of atonal thrusts and electronic feedback. The lyrics combine sado-masochistic frenzy with free association imagery. The whole sound seems to be the product of a secret marriage between Bob Dylan and the Marquis de Sade.
RICHARD GOLDSTEIN, *NEW YORK WORLD JOURNAL-TRIBUNE*, 1966

ANDY WARHOL

There we were in the Moulin Rouge. It was a dark night. He'd come by camel. I came by taxi. No, we were playing a tourist trap in Greenwich Village called the Café Bizarre and some friends asked Andy to come and see us and thought that he might like us. And he saw us. He thought it was great. But Andy thinks everything's great. He had a week at the Cinematheque to show his movies, so he said, 'Why don't you come?' He would show his movies on us. And we did. And that makes mixed media. We wore black so you could see the movie. But we were all wearing black anyway.
LOU REED, APRIL 1979

It sounds crazy, but on reflection I've decided that he was never wrong. He gave us the confidence to keep doing what we were doing.
STERLING MORRISON, APRIL 1981

He was a spy, he spied on everybody. He put disparate elements together, which is what I've always appreciated him for, because it's what I try to do with music.
JOHN CALE, SEPTEMBER 1985

Andy Warhol, whose hair was silver . . . was everything I had expected, looking exactly as he did in the gossip column pictures: the shades, the polo neck, the mask. I cannot recall what was said or even that anything was said at all.
KEN PITT, *THE PITT REPORT*, 1983

I'm not involved with Warhol at all, now. He might say something to me that might make a good line in a song. Like, I didn't have the lyrics for 'Sunday Morning' and he said, 'Why don't you make it a song about paranoia?' I thought that was great so I came up with, 'Watch out, the world is behind you, there is always someone watching you', which I feel is the ultimate paranoid statement in that the world even cares enough to watch you.
LOU REED, MAY 1973

He was an influence in suggesting that everybody has magic, so if mistakes happen on stage they can work and become part of the show.
JOHN CALE, MAY 1975

The atmosphere of Warhol's circus seems to have suited Lou, the craziness of its larger-than-death characters, only too aware of the futility that passed for normal life, offering nothing themselves but that awareness dressed up as style. And who but Warhol would have had both the money and the desire to stage The Velvet Underground with their patently outrageous music?
DAVID DOWNING, *FUTURE ROCK*, 1976

I love Andy. He's always understood where I'm coming from. Years ago he said that I was to be to music what he was to the visual arts. You can't define it, but it's all happening just the way he said it would. The man's amazing. He's also always said to me that work is the most important thing in a man's life and I believe him. My work is my yoga. It empties me out.
LOU REED, JUNE 1977

He would rather be me or someone else sometimes . . . like the radio interview when I couldn't show up . . . he went on and took my part – said the things I would say.
NICO, 1966

At the time, The Velvet Underground seemed to reflect his thing, although it was no more his thing than ours. People would say, 'Warhol's taken over your mind', but it was so silly. All the songs for the first album were written before I met Andy. But for years after, everyone thought we were like soup cans, a Warhol put on. We credited him so heavily because we knew it would get more attention that way. At the time it was his supermarket, so we were happy to be a soup can. He still seems to like my music. He always comes to the concerts and takes a real interest.
LOU REED, JUNE 1977

The pop idea, after all, was that anybody could do anything, so naturally we were all trying to do it all. Nobody wanted to stay in one category, we all wanted to branch out into every creative thing we could. That's why when we met The Velvet Underground at the end of '65, we were all for getting into the music scene, too.
ANDY WARHOL, 1983

I enjoyed my time with Andy Warhol, it was tremendous. It made me cry a lot. We had conflicts, Lou and I and John and I, we had conflicts and I like conflicts.
NICO, MARCH 1975

What kind of man would paint a Campbell's soup can?
DAVID BOWIE, 1972

Andy Warhol – the camera is a man's best friend.

THE FACTORY

The Factory, Andy Warhol's now famous studio, was high up in an old industrial building on East 47th Street. To get to the upper floors, one had to risk one's life by travelling in a rickety goods lift that was nothing more than a large cage, rather like the ones coal miners use to descend to the depths. It wasn't in a well, as are conventional lifts, and you could look out on three sides to a sheer drop to the ground.
KEN PITT, *THE PITT REPORT*, 1983

We used to practise at The Factory and hang out there every day for a couple of years, from '66 to '68. We would arrive some time in the afternoon and every day would begin with the same question, 'What parties shall we go to tonight?' We even went to one with Nelson Rockefeller. I thought, if Delmore could see me now.
STERLING MORRISON, APRIL 1981

THE VELVET UNDER-GROUND -THE GROUP (II)

The Velvet Underground were so far ahead of their time that hearing them now it seems scarcely believable that they're not a contemporary group.
LYNDEN BARBER, *MELODY MAKER*, DECEMBER 1983

The Velvet Underground were the first avant-garde rock band, and the greatest.
MARY HARRON, *NME*, APRIL 1981

I was very, very taken aback that people were surprised when The Velvet Underground very consciously set out to put themes common to movies, plays and novels into pop song format. For Godsakes, you know, take these poppy lyrics out and put these other ones in, in the same style of course, and then just see the horrified reaction.
LOU REED, MAY 1983

The Velvets were so loud and crazy I couldn't even begin to guess the decibels, and there were images projected everywhere, one on top of the other. I'd usually watch from the balcony or take my turn at the projectors, slipping different coloured gelatin slides over the lenses and turning movies like *Harlot, The Shoplifter, Couch, Banana, Blow Job, Sleep* . . . into all different colours.
ANDY WARHOL, 1983

I didn't appreciate what we were doing. I never considered what it meant to be doing something with Andy Warhol and seeing all these weird people marching by and hanging around the loft. I just worried about little songs and how well they were played.
STERLING MORRISON, APRIL 1981

When Andy picked up on us there was nothing else like it going down. We used to have a whole theatrical trip, with whips and dancers and Andy or Paul Morrissey doing the lights. Paul had some really weird films in those days, and I was always trying to get him to let us show them. But he wouldn't. There really was an underground in those days, with a whole mess of people involved. It just hasn't been like that for years.
LOU REED, JUNE 1977

I always found myself caught between playing viola and playing bass. I never thought we made enough of the viola, which is a very powerful instrument.
JOHN CALE, APRIL 1974

There were always conflicts and presumably there always will be. Lou was the vocalist, front man and songwriter for the band. I was just taking it easy and generally having fun. Now I look back on it all I wasn't particularly enamoured of the more garish aspects of, say, the Exploding Plastic Inevitable row, but then that's exactly what Lou was very into.
JOHN CALE, APRIL 1974

In the days of The Velvet Underground, recording engineers would hear what we did and leave. They'd say, 'I'll come back when you've finished', turn on the tape machine and go. So I got this attitude that engineers were my enemy and the way we recorded reflected that. I'd have the band play the song for the first time in the studio, I'd maybe make up lyrics as we went along and the whole thing would go down on tape sounding as natural and spontaneous as possible.
LOU REED, AUGUST 1984

I really did very little with The Velvets. I just look back on all that as a fixed period of time which was very educational in its way but my musical contribution was, I felt, quite minimal.
JOHN CALE, APRIL 1974

The flowers of evil are in full bloom with The Exploding Plastic Inevitable.
MICHAELO WILLIAMS, *CHICAGO DAILY NEWS*, 1966

I heard a bootleg tape of a concert we did at Columbus, Ohio, and all it sounded like was Lou constantly tuning his guitar up and down for 10 minutes at a time and, absolutely no applause.
JOHN CALE, APRIL 1974

Lou and John, on stage at The Paris
Bataclan in 1971.

I wrote no songs myself. I was intimidated by Lou. And because I was intimidated, I probably over-reacted and forced the arranging side of things.
JOHN CALE, MAY 1975

We never cared that much about touring. We did it once in a while by invitation, but we never solicited one. Why play Toledo, Ohio, where no one knows you and where people are not likely to be the least bit receptive? Deep down you do want to be accepted by audiences; I don't care how much you steel yourself with drugs or whatever.
STERLING MORRISON, APRIL 1981

I was just a sideman. Though I guess there was a dramatic situation when I broke my wrist and played with a cast on it. To play with a cast on your arm you have to look really cunty. The whole point of The Velvet Underground was never to do a concert the same twice, because of Lou's ability to make up lyrics. 'Sister Ray Part Two' was amazing, some of the things Lou was making up.
JOHN CALE, AUGUST 1975

We had a horrible reputation. Everyone figured we were gay. They figured we must be, running around with Warhol and all those whips and stuff.
STERLING MORRISON, APRIL 1981

In The Velvet Underground the idea was to go out there and improvise songs on stage. I talked to Andy Warhol about it and he said we should actually go out there and rehearse. Like, stop and go back and teach each other and the audience the songs. It really sucks attention in. Like Orson Wells in his movies, he would have dialogue with four people speaking simultaneously, which meant you really had to pay attention. That kind of gripping element, that style of working really sucks people in.
JOHN CALE, APRIL 1981

We would practise the beginning and the end of a song; as we never played it the same way twice it didn't matter if we practised the middle. If there was anything weird about it then we went over that. But the songs we practised the most, the really polished songs, we never recorded. We knew we could do them, so there was no more interest. We wanted to see if we could make something else work. Our best stuff, about 80 per cent of it, was either radically reworked in the studio, or written there.
STERLING MORRISON, APRIL 1981

The unanimous opinion was that we were 10 times better live than we were on our records.
STERLING MORRISON, APRIL 1981

The Velvet Underground had a heavy Germanic influence. Nico was from Cologne, close where we live. They have this German dada influence from the twenties and thirties. I very much like 'European Son'. Nico and John Cale have this Teutonic attitude about their music which I very much like.
FLORIAN, KRAFTWERK, SEPTEMBER 1975

Stuck out here (Tucson, Arizona) in the middle of nowhere the only friends we have are my husband's, from work. But quite a few of them have heard of The Velvets, and they're impressed.
MO TUCKER, MAY 1981

I don't feel any nostalgia for The Velvet Underground. I can't even remember most of what went on. God, they were primitive times. Driving round in a Winnebego van, being stopped by the police and being accused of child kidnapping because the girls we had with us were too young and they didn't have notes from their parents. God they were primitive times. We were right in the middle of Ohio, taking speed, driving all the way back from Cleveland to New York overnight. Madness.
JOHN CALE, FEBRUARY 1983

I didn't really think about my years with The Velvets much until recently, when the climate seemed the same again. With New Wave the music went back to the people who were kind of screwing around on records, who knew they couldn't possibly achieve mass appeal, and didn't care. I was looking at all these little punk bands and thinking, 'Well, there goes us again.'
STERLING MORRISON, APRIL 1981

LIGHTS ... ACTION ...

Anyone in the audience could come up and work the lights. We never had things like, 'When I play this 10 second break, then hit me with the blue spot.' That's what I hate about modern rock shows. They're so regimented. We just played and everything raged about us without any control on our part.
STERLING MORRISON, APRIL 1981

We actually built the light show at the Fillmore. Bill Graham didn't, nor did any San Francisco entrepreneur. When we showed up, Graham had a slide projector with a picture of the moon. We said, 'That's not a light show, Bill, sorry.' That's one of the reasons that Graham really hates us.
STERLING MORRISON, 1983

The guy who was doing our lights committed suicide eventually. Danny Williams. The strobes we were using in The Exploding Plastic Inevitable, he would sit for hours up at the Factory, all that aluminium, seven strobe lights, and you can imagine. He used himself as a test subject. John and I, that's why we used to wear sunglasses. We didn't want to see it. We knew, and Danny, he was so far gone he killed himself.
LOU REED, JANUARY 1976

As far as wearing sunglasses on stage, the only reason we wore them was we couldn't stand the sight of the audience.
JOHN CALE, SEPTEMBER 1985

Andy Warhol and Legs McNeil.

... NOISE (THE EAST VILLAGE OTHER ELECTRIC NEWSPAPER)

Unfortunately, (The Velvets) only got to play for about a minute, and the blaring radio broadcast of Luci Johnson's wedding which runs through the whole record all but drowns them out. Not only that, but it's set stereo centre, so you can't turn out one speaker to fully absorb that brief moment of primal Velvets.
LESTER BANGS, *CREEM*, DECEMBER 1971

If there exists beauty so universal as to be unquestionable, Nico possesses it.
GERARD MALANGA, 1967

As a fashion model in Paris I wanted to be a singer. But you have to learn how to sing. It's just required. You can't be a ballet dancer or a trapeze artist without having learnt it, you can't just jump on a trapeze and not fall, or break your neck.
NICO, MARCH 1975

Nico's the kind of person you meet, and you're not quite the same afterwards. She has an amazing mind. She isn't the type of person who stays long in any country. Nico's fantastic.
LOU REED, 1983

Nico was great. She taught me how to eat pussy, me a skinny naïve little brat, she taught me all about French wine and German champagne, and one day she said, 'Jimmy. You have one big problem. You are not full of poison. How can you perform if you are not full of poison? We don't want to see a person on the stage, we want to see a performance, and poison is the essence of the performer.' And I used to go away and come back looking really healthy and she'd scream, 'Jimmy, what are you doing to yourself? You are ugly! You are only good skinny.' Then Danny Fields used to start fussing with my hair in his usual faggy way and he and Nico used to have these rows about it. My hair was really long and curly. He wanted it cut, Nico thought it was better if it hid my face completely. She drew this picture of me with all this hair, two cubic inches of my face showing. And she got Danny and everybody and said, 'This is all you want to see of Jimmy's face. This is Jimmy's face. If you could see the rest of it it would be a drag.' And I thought, 'Right on, Nico.'
IGGY POP, 1977

I met Nico in New York. She was really lovely and we were like boyfriend and girlfriend for a while. I told her, 'I have to go to Michigan to be with the band' – being Michigan boys they never really had any interest in being anywhere but near Detroit – and she said, 'Jimmy, I go with you.' She spoke like that. And I thought, 'What is a sophisticated lady like her, what does she want to do out where I am? She must be nuts.' She was, and I owe her the world.
IGGY POP, *I NEED MORE*, 1983

They think I'm not polite . . . but whatever I have to say to these people seems so unnecessary. I just can't be around . . . anything that is forced. I'd rather just remain how I feel . . . what happened before happened. Now it's only the sentiment that you can't scratch out.
NICO, 1966

She'd try to cook for us. She'd cook pots of brown rice every day and sometimes serve fresh fruit, but mainly brown rice and vegetables. She'd try to cook for us. She'd cook brown rice in a pot and throw vegetables in, and it would always have so much tabasco and hot sauce that nobody could eat it, but she tried.
IGGY POP, *I NEED MORE*, 1983

I haven't time to be a cliché.
NICO, APRIL 1978

Iggy Pop.

LA DOLCE VITA

Ah Nico, the old cow. Sure she looks old and 38 and her face is drawn, but Nico will always be the role she played in *La Dolce Vita* for me – a German cow having her face slapped.
JOHN CALE, SEPTEMBER 1977

I was living in Rome at the time and I was friends with an actress called Silvana Mangano. She is a professional gambler, she plays roulette very well. I liked gambling a lot although I don't know how to do it. There was Fellini and her and her husband and her children and all her friends. Fellini kept me in a house all the time, and he promised me a part in the movie. I don't know why he promised me a part, he thought that I wanted to be in one. I didn't beg him to be in that, I just asked him to be in it.
NICO, MARCH 1975

THE LAST MILE

I was appearing on a *Ready Steady Go* programme and that's where I think I met Andrew Oldham, maybe I'd met him before, I don't know. It was through Brian Jones I met Andrew. Andrew wrote 'The Last Mile', and one song, the first side, was a Gordon Lightfoot song, 'I'm Not Saying'.
NICO, MARCH 1975

LEONARD COHEN

She's incredible. She's a great singer and a great songwriter. Completely disregarded from what I can see. I don't think she sells 50 records, but she's one of the really original talents in the whole racket.
LEONARD COHEN, OCTOBER 1974

I was very taken by Nico . . . she was singing at La Dom, which was an Andy Warhol club on 8th Street. I just stumbled in there one night and I didn't know any of these people. I saw this girl singing behind the bar. She was a sight to behold. I suppose the most beautiful woman I'd ever seen up to that moment. I just walked up and stood in front of her until people pushed me aside. I started writing songs for her then.
LEONARD COHEN, OCTOBER 1974

He came to see me at La Dom every night. And we both ate the same kind of food – well, he turned me on to that kind of food at the time, macrobiotic things.
NICO, MARCH 1975

Nico introduced me to Lou Reed and Lou Reed surprised me greatly because he had a book of my poems. I hadn't been published in America, and I had a very small audience even in Canada. So when Lou Reed asked me to sign *Flowers For Hitler*, I thought it was an extremely friendly gesture of his. He played me his songs. It was the first time I heard them. I thought they were excellent – really fine. I used to praise him. I can't say I know him well at all. He was an early reader of *Beautiful Losers* which he thought was a good book. In those days I guess he wasn't getting very many compliments for his work and I certainly wasn't. So we told each other how good we were.
LEONARD COHEN, OCTOBER 1974

Canadian Leonard Cohen, whose "Joan of Arc" was apparently written or Nico.

LA DOM

That was the only club I ever sang at. I would never sing in a club ever again, because of the great memories of that. It wasn't very easy with all the drunks that came in and asked me if I wanted a drink while I was singing. Sometimes I had to be very rude. I was singing, you know, and a person would come up to me and say, 'Would you like some champagne? Here baby, have a drink.' It was almost like The Blue Angel, the same kind of situation.
NICO, MARCH 1975

THE VELVET UNDER- GROUND WITH NICO

I'd been living in New York since 1959, modelling – modelling for Fords, until I took up acting lessons with Lee Strasbourg. Marilyn Monroe was in my class. It was very exciting. Andy said I should join him in New York and it was Bob Dylan who introduced me to Andy, and he also told Andy he should make movies with me.
NICO, SEPTEMBER 1985

Nico is astonishing – the macabre face – so beautifully resembling a *momento mori*, the marvellous death-like voice coming from the lovely blonde head.
DAVID ANTRIM, *ART NEWS*, 1966

There were problems from the very beginning, because there were only so many songs that were appropriate for Nico and she wanted to sing them all – 'Waiting For The Man', 'Heroin', all of them. And she would try and do little sexual politics things in the band. Whoever seemed to be having undue influence on the course of events, you'd find Nico close to them. So she went from Lou to Cale, but neither of those affairs lasted very long.
STERLING MORRISON, APRIL 1981

I felt that the one thing The Velvets didn't have was a solo singer, because I just didn't think Lou had the personality to stand in front of the group and sing. The group needed something beautiful to counteract the screeching ugliness they were trying to sell, and the combination of a beautiful girl standing in front of all this decadence was what was needed.
PAUL MORRISSEY, 1983

Andy suggested we use Nico as a vocalist. She'd made a couple of singles with Andrew Oldham in London, and one of them was not bad – sort of like early Marianne Faithful. So we said fine, she looks great, and just gradually tried to work her in.
STERLING MORRISON, APRIL 1981

Lou didn't want her on the album. Lou was always jealous of Nico and he only let her sing little songs on the album, then he wrote a song for her called 'Sunday Morning' and wouldn't let her sing it.
PAUL MORRISSEY, 1983

I really had very little to do with her in The Velvets. Lou fell madly in love with her, wrote lots of songs and was absolutely torn up by it all of course.
JOHN CALE, APRIL 1974

Nico had two voices. One was a full register Germanic, gotterdammerung voice that I never cared for, and the other was her whispery voice, that I liked. But it's not because she was singing to Lou Reed or Bob Dylan or anybody. Nico was really depressed.
STERLING MORRISON, APRIL 1981

Lou wrote the greatest songs for her to sing, like 'Femme Fatale', 'I'll Be Your Mirror', 'All Tomorrow's Parties'. Her voice, the words, and the sounds The Velvets made were all so magical together.
ANDY WARHOL, 1983

We most certainly did not want to be associated with Dylan. We did not want to be near Dylan, either physically or through his songs. When Nico kept insisting that we work up 'I'll Keep It With Mine', for a long time we simply refused. Then we took a long time to learn it, as long as we could take. After that, even though we knew the song, we insisted that we were unable to play it. When we finally did have a go at it on-stage, it was performed poorly. We never got any better at it either, for some reason.
STERLING MORRISON, 1983

Her voice is low but strong, sensuous but reserved. Sometimes she seems as if she is talking to herself.
PAT PATTERSON, *IN*, 1966

Dylan was always sneaking around giving Nico songs to sing.
JOHN CALE, SEPTEMBER 1985

I stopped modelling when I felt that it didn't interest me any longer to look at myself in the mirror all the time. If you do it all the time for a living it becomes no longer fun. It becomes absurd.
NICO, MARCH 1975

The first album, the whole thing, was done in a day at Cameo Parkway Studios. I remember they were tearing down the walls, ripping up the floorboards, the whole place was a shambles. They charged us $1,500 and threw in an engineer. We thought it was very reasonable of them.
JOHN CALE, FEBRUARY 1983

I love the Banana album so much. It's so innocent. Everybody was saying this is the vision of all-time evil and I always said, well we're not going to lie. It's pretty. 'Venus In Furs' is a beautiful song. It was the closest we ever came in my mind to being exactly what I always thought we could be. Always on the other songs I'm hearing what I'm hearing, but I'm also hearing what I wish I was hearing.
STERLING MORRISON, APRIL 1981

"I want to sound like Bawb Dee- Lahn."
(Nico, 1967)

'Venus In Furs' is my favourite. Musically it's so shocking, that's what frightened people. It could have been about anything.
STERLING MORRISON, SEPTEMBER 1985

The whole time the album was being made, nobody seemed happy with it, especially Nico. 'I want to sound like Bawwwhhhb Deee-lahhhn' she wailed, so upset because she didn't.
ANDY WARHOL, 1983

The album says, 'Produced by Andy Warhol'. Well, it was produced in the sense that a movie is produced. He put up some money. We made the album ourselves and then took it around because we knew that no one was going to sign us off the streets. And we didn't want any A & R department telling us what songs we should record. Ahmet Ertegun liked it, but said, 'No no no, none of this – no 'Waiting For The Man', no 'Venus In Furs'.' Then we took it over to Elektra, who said some of the content was unacceptable, and the whole sound was unacceptable. 'This viola – can't Cale play anything else?' The album was ready by April 1966, but I don't think it even made a '66 release, or at least not until the end of the year. We were going crazy wondering what was going on while things got lost and misplaced and delayed. I know what the problem was. It was Frank Zappa and his manager, Herb Cohen. They sabotaged us in a number of ways, because they wanted to be first with a freak release. And we were totally naïve. We didn't have a manager who would go to the record company every day and just drag the whole thing through production.
STERLING MORRISON, APRIL 1981

We'd actually worked very hard on the arrangements for the first album. We used to meet once a week for about a year, just working on arrangements.
JOHN CALE, FEBRUARY 1983

The first album . . . it turned out to be prophetic, but there was no way of knowing at the time.
ROBERT CHRISTGAU, SEPTEMBER 1985

At the start we had 'Heroin', 'Waiting For The Man' and 'Venus In Furs', all on the first album, and that just about set the tone. We also had 'Sunday Morning', which was so pretty, and 'I'll Be Your Mirror', but everyone psyched into the other stuff. The prosaic truth about 'Venus In Furs' is that I'd just read this book by Sacher-Masoch, and I thought it would make a great song title, so I had to write a song to go with it. But it's not necessarily what I'm into.
LOU REED, JUNE 1977

I think we all had the idea to have a nice, amateur sound on the record. All the amps would be on at the same time, of course, there'd be feedback and hissing and stuff which you really don't hear, but if you took it away you'd notice the difference.
MO TUCKER, SEPTEMBER 1985

'Heroin' is very close to the feeling you get from smack. It starts on a certain level, it's deceptive. You think you're enjoying it. But by the time it hits you, it's too late. You don't have any choice. It comes at you harder and faster and it keeps on coming. The song is everything but the real thing is doing it to you.
LOU REED, JUNE 1977

The lyrics to 'Heroin' certainly were not self-pitying.
JOHN CALE, SEPTEMBER 1985

They're good songs, they're gonna sound good no matter who plays them, but they're nothing like the way we played them, me with my no drum training just bashing away, Sterling with his nice, quiet little ideas of guitar playing and his real solid rhythm playing, and John with his manic viola. Lou would go off on a tangent and Cale would go off on a tangent and if somebody wasn't holding it all down it would all be just a mess of confusion, so I would concentrate on just playing the same beat as we started at, so that when everybody came back there was something to go back to.
MO TUCKER, SEPTEMBER 1985

They wouldn't even accept advertising for the album, because it was about drugs and perversion and sex. So we said, 'Fuck 'em, if they're not going to play us on the radio, we're not going to play there.' It was a good way to generate mystique, but that wasn't our intention. We wanted to punish New York.
STERLING MORRISON, APRIL 1981

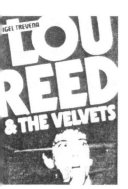

THE VELVET UNDERGROUND WITHOUT NICO

They had some personality problems, they wanted to get rid of me because I had more attention in the press. Well, that's how it went.
NICO, MARCH 1975

BRIAN EPSTEIN

I wanted Brian to manage them or promote them or get them to Europe or just something. At least I turned him on to them, which is something. It was high time Europe heard them. In fact, he did go back, I understand, and when people asked him what was happening in America he would say you should go listen to that album.
DANNY FIELDS, 1983

Brian Epstein built an empire and lived long enough to have a lot of time on his hands.
LOU REED, *FALLEN KNIGHTS AND FALLEN LADIES*, 1974

One night at Max's I was there with Brian Epstein and Lou Reed was there and I ran back and said, 'Pretend you have to go uptown and I'll get you a ride with Brian Epstein.' Prior to this, when I had first told Brian about The Velvet Underground, he had gone out and bought their record and then he left for Acapulco for a week and it was the only record he had with him, the banana album, he lived with it for a week. So I ran back and said to Brian, 'Could you drop me at Ondines and Lou Reed as well', and he said 'Sure.' In the car Brian said, 'Well, I've certainly been listening to your record a great deal', and Louis said 'Oh?', and Brian said, 'Well, I liked it very much', and Lou said, 'Why, thank you.'
DANNY FIELDS, 1974

Brian Epstein – the original
Fallen Knight.

We had a lot of dealings with Brian Epstein. He loved the first album and it was his favourite record for a long time. We had a lot of talks with him, riding in his car around Manhattan. First he wanted to sign us and have us be his only American group. But he managed a lot of groups and he never let them threaten The Beatles. So we refused.
STERLING MORRISON, APRIL 1981

WHITE LIGHT

The Velvets, for all the seeming crudity of their music, were interested in the possibilities of noise right from the start, and had John Cale's extensive conservatory training to help shape their experiments. By the time (they) recorded 'Sister Ray' they seemed to have carried their Yardbirds/Who project to its ultimate extension.
LESTER BANGS, NOVEMBER 1970

When I was living in the loft it was just me, a bed, and our stuff . . . five or six huge amplifiers and guitars. And I could hook 'em all in series. We'd come flying in at five in the morning and play 'Sister Ray' through them. I was the only guy living in the building, except for this junkie upstairs. He used to jump up and down on the floor when we got going.
LOU REED, JANUARY 1976

Lou never did anything like that after I left the band. But I don't know. Those guitar solos are all Lou's, and one of them, I think it's on 'I Heard Her Call My Name', is really incredible. But that was his sound.
JOHN CALE, APRIL 1974

When we did 'Sister Ray' we turned up to 10 flat out, leakage all over the place. That's it. They asked us what we were going to do. We said we're going to start. They said, 'Who's playing the bass?' We said there is no bass. They asked us when it ends? We didn't know. When it ends, that's when it ends.
LOU REED, JANUARY 1976

The albums sound awful to me in some respects. They're really badly recorded.
JOHN CALE, FEBRUARY 1983

We didn't want to lay down separate tracks, we wanted to do it studio live with a simultaneous voice, but the problem was that the current state of studio art wouldn't let us do it. There was fantastic leakage because everyone was playing so loud and we had so much electronic junk with us in the studio – all these fuzzers and compressors. Gary Kellgran the engineer, who is ultra-competent, told us repeatedly, 'You can't do it – all the needles are on red.' And we reacted as we always reacted: 'Look, we don't know what goes on in there and we don't want to hear about it. Just do the best you can.' And so the album is all fuzzy, there's all that white noise.
STERLING MORRISON, APRIL 1981

All those songs are so fast. I kept trying to get them down to a slightly slower pace, y'know? They would have sounded better. 'The Gift' came about after we'd recorded this instrumental we always did as a warm-up number when we played live, called 'The Booker T'. It went on for about 12 minutes and we thought that was no good, so Lou produced one of his short stories and got me to read it. He'd just written a number of these stories at the time and they were all very good. Very simple and direct.
JOHN CALE, APRIL 1974

'White Light' was all energy, the result of our experiences as a road band. Being on the road, we soon realised people were there to dance, so we started playing rock 'n' roll. But no one had any patience any more to work on arrangements and it shows. We just went into the studios, turned the amps as high as we could and blasted away. Everyone's nerves were frazzled by then, we were rabid. That's when I decided to go.
JOHN CALE, FEBRUARY 1983

No producer could override our taste. We'd do a whole lot of takes, and then there would be a big brawl over which one to use. Of course, everyone would opt for the take where they sounded best. It was a tremendous hassle, so on 'Sister Ray', which we knew was going to be a major effort, we stared at each other and said, 'This is going to be one take. So whatever you want to do, you better do it now.' And that explains what's going on in the mix. Everyone's trying to do what he wants to do every second, and no one backs off. I think it's great the way the organ comes in. Cale starts to try and play a solo. He's totally buried and there's a sort of surge and then he's pulling out all the stops until he just rises out of the pack. He was able to get louder than Lou and I were. The drums were almost totally drowned out.
STERLING MORRISON, APRIL 1981

SUCKING ON MY DING DONG

I would suck Lou Reed's cock, because I would also kiss the feet of them that drafted the Magna Carta.
LESTER BANGS, 1980

CALE QUITS!

Lou called Mo and I to a meeting to announce that Cale was out. I said, you mean out for today or for this week? And Lou said, 'No, he's out.' I said that we were the band, that was it, graven on the tablets. So then there was a long and bitter argument, with much banging on tables and finally Lou said, 'You don't go for it? All right, the band is dissolved.' Now I could say that it was more important to keep the band together than to worry about Cale, but that wasn't really what decided me. I just wanted to keep on doing it. So finally I weighed my self-interest against Cale's interests and sold him out. I told Lou I'd swallow it, but I didn't really like it.
STERLING MORRISON, APRIL 1981

I'd just got married, which was one cause, I think. Also, Lou was starting to act funny. He brought in this guy called Selznick – who I thought was a real snake – to be our manager and all this intrigue started to take place. Lou was calling us 'his band' while Selznick was trying to get him to go solo. I dunno, maybe it was the drugs he was doing at the time. They certainly didn't help.
JOHN CALE, APRIL 1974

Lou played me this song he'd written and I immediately started adding an improvised viola part. Sterling muttered something about it being a good viola part and Lou turned round and said, 'Yeah I know. I wrote the song just for that viola part. Every single note of it I knew in advance.'
JOHN CALE, APRIL 1974

It was jealousy, I'd have to say. One friend said Lou told him he wanted to be a solo star. Lou never confided that to us, but John and I always knew that he really wanted some kind of recognition apart from the band.
STERLING MORRISON, APRIL 1981

It was sad in a way because there were still some great songs to be recorded, like 'Here Comes The Waves' which later became 'The Ocean' on his first solo album and a bunch of others.
JOHN CALE, APRIL 1974

DOUG YULE

I liked him. I was a little concerned because I went to Louie's loft on 28th and 7th by Penn Station to help rehearse one evening. Doug had just worked out a bass-part to 'Jesus' and when I came in, Louie said 'Listen to this, it's great, it's great', and I thought, 'Oh God, don't swell this kid's head before he even gets out in the street.'
MO TUCKER, 1983

THE VELVET UNDER-GROUND
THE THIRD ALBUM

'Pale Blue Eyes' – that's a song about Lou's old girlfriend in Syracuse. I said, 'Lou, if I wrote a song like that I wouldn't make you play it.' My position on that album was one of acquiescence.
STERLING MORRISON, APRIL 1981

Sterling's a pain in the ass!
MO TUCKER, 1983

I guess that's around the time Sterling was beginning to get disgusted with Lou, pissed off, whatever the word is, why, I don't know. It had a lot to do with them being males, I suppose. I know that sounds tacky, but I've thought a lot about it and I think it has a lot to do with it, ego problems and all. I just found it totally acceptable if Lou was being crazy, or being a pain in the ass, to say, 'Oh well' and forget it, whereas Sterling couldn't do that.
MO TUCKER, 1983

The main reason for Doug doing the vocals is that Lou's voice wasn't up to it when we were in the studio. Lou never had a durable voice, which is one of the reasons we tried not to play too often. Lou had used up his voice at the Whiskey where we played during the time we were making the album. Since we wanted to get the album finished, and since Doug could sing, he got the nod.
STERLING MORRISON, 1981

Doug had a sweet little voice and he could sing certain songs better than Lou.
MO TUCKER, 1983

We did the third album deliberately as anti-production. It sounds like it was done in a closet. It's flat and that's the way we wanted it. The songs are all very quiet and it's kind of insane. I like the album.
STERLING MORRISON, APRIL 1981

I never saw any reviews. I was pleased with the direction we were going and with the new calmness in the group, and thinking about a good future, hoping people would smarten up and some record company would take us on and do us justice.
MO TUCKER, 1983

I dismissed decadence when I did 'The Murder Mystery'.
LOU REED, MARCH 1975

The Velvet Underground have closed their career as the aging darlings of the avant-garde. Instead, they released a third album studded with prayerful diamonds of songs, invoked Jesus, saw the light, dispelled the shadows of heroin and speed.
ROBERT GREENFIELD, MARCH 1970

The band was never the same for me after John left. He was not easy to replace. Doug Yule was a good bass player, but we moved more towards unanimity of opinion, and I don't think that's a good thing. I always thought that what made us really good were the tensions and oppositions. Cale's departure allowed Lou's sensitive, meaningful side out. Why do you think that happened on the third album?
STERLING MORRISON, APRIL 1981

The first time I saw them they were awful, the second time they were fairly great.
JUDY SIMS, *MELODY MAKER*, 1969

We've never had a hit and only had two moderately successful albums.
DOUG YULE, 1969

THE GREAT LOST VELVETS ALBUM

I have some dubs of it. It was done some time in early '69. That's the stuff Lou drew on when he went solo. Nearly everything on his first album was just a reworking of stuff he'd already done.
STERLING MORRISON, APRIL 1981

Electricity comes from other planets.
LOU REED, 'INSIDE YOUR HEART', 1969

LIVE 1969

The 'Sweet Jane' on the Mercury 'Live 1969' album, that's 'Sweet Jane'. The original lyrics, even recorded the way I wrote it.
LOU REED, JANUARY 1976

That version, I think that night was the first night we'd played it. Some rich kid in Texas had a sort of club. If he liked a group, he'd bring them into the club and invite friends over. It was insane.
LOU REED, JANUARY 1976

It was because of 'Rock 'n' Roll Animal' that the '1969' album was able to come out.
LOU REED, JANUARY 1976

The legendary Max's, scene of The Velvets' last stand, in August, 1970.

LIVE AT MAX'S

I've always arranged it so bootlegs could come out. The Max's set, now that's the other album I love. If you want to know what Max's was really like – and now you can't – but there, for real . . . because Brigid (Polk) was just sitting there with her little Sony recorder. It's in mono, you can't hear it, but you can hear just enough. We're out of tune, as per usual, but it's Sunday night and all the regulars are there, and Jim Carroll's trying to get tuinols and they're talking about the war and we were the house band. There it is.
LOU REED, JANUARY 1976

LOADED

In 1970 Ahmet Ertegun asked us to tour. We said, 'Fine, you start the promotion and then we'll start the tour.' He said, 'No, you start the tour and then we'll start the promotion.' So we went skiing instead.
STERLING MORRISON, APRIL 1981

Those old rock 'n' roll songs where the guy'll start talking and go, 'Honey'. I did that with 'I Found A Reason'.
LOU REED, APRIL 1982

I had a significant influence on Lou. Lou and I had a significant influence together on the group. I, of course, did no more than Lou – he was doing the writing, I was arranger, musical director. I was handling my half, he was handling his. Many said Lou was The Velvet Underground, and in the sense that it was his brainchild, he was. He was the main force behind it, but it was a band and like any band its totality is made up of all its members, not just one person with side musicians.
DOUG YULE, 1983

LOU LEAVES

I gave them an album loaded with hits and it was loaded with hits to the point where the rest of the people showed their colours. So I left them to their album full of hits that I made.
LOU REED, JULY 1973

Lou was acting very oddly. He told me he was leaving the group, he was really really upset and we sat there for a time, I didn't put any questions to him or argue, he had obviously made his decision. He didn't give me any specific reasons, and that was the last night he played with us.
MO TUCKER, SEPTEMBER 1985

We had really all already gone our separate ways. I didn't have any communication with any of them except Maureen.
LOU REED, SEPTEMBER 1985

If I hadn't quit The Velvet Underground, I'd be loaded. Loaded! If I hadn't quit the group when I did we would have broken. We'd have made it.
LOU REED, DECEMBER 1976

SQUEEZE THE VELVET UNDERGROUND

That time was very pleasant. We were working on new songs and we sounded very good. But when I looked at myself I was seeing a professional musician which I never really set out to be. There wasn't the old excitement, the feeling of crusading.
STERLING MORRISON, APRIL 1981

REPACKAGING THE LEGEND . . .

I kept going with 'Rock 'n' Roll Animal' because it did what it was supposed to do. It got the '1969' album out, it got MGM to repackage all those Velvets things. Now they've repackaged it 700 different ways, and we still don't see any royalties, but that isn't the point.
LOU REED, JANUARY 1976

They leave out a lot of the heavy stuff. It's always 'Sister Ray', it's always 'Heroin' . . . and I'm really glad they're on it. You can hear what we were doing 11 years ago.
LOU REED, JANUARY 1976

. . . AND RECYCLING IT:
PRAETORIAN UNDERGROUND

The cult of The Velvet Underground is distasteful to me. I mean, all the promise we showed in those two albums, we never delivered on it. I'm sure Lou feels the same way. He's as stubborn and egocentric as I am.
JOHN CALE, FEBRUARY 1983

It's like being a bar of soap in a shower that doesn't have any water in it. It doesn't work. Being a living legend is such a precarious livelihood.
JOHN CALE, MARCH 1984

Bowie played 'White Light' and 'Waiting For The Man', which was the first time I'd ever heard anybody acknowledge The Velvet Underground.
KRIS NEEDS, SEPTEMBER 1984

'The Len Bright Combo' . . . can quite reasonably claim to be the worst recorded record since The Velvets first turned everything up full blast and played till the recording heads broke.
DAVE THOMPSON, *MELODY MAKER*, MARCH 1986

Everybody's talking about this band The Velvet Underground influencing this and that. They're even saying Talking Heads are reminiscent of The Velvet Underground, which has absolutely nothing to do with what we sounded like. And many of the people making these assessments and writing these reviews never saw us live. All they've got to go by are live reissues by Lou Reed, that kind of narcissistic nepotism. He just regenerates the same material over and over again, in different form.
JOHN CALE, APRIL 1981

A lot of people who talk about The Velvet Underground never even heard us. I think The Velvets are dead and well underground by now.
JOHN CALE, SEPTEMBER 1979

After us, the perfect record is 'I Wanna Be Your Dog' by The Stooges, but the horrible guitar solo fucked it up. 'Heroin' by The Velvet Underground is almost perfect, but I don't like the violin.
WILLIAM REID, NOVEMBER 1985

I know it sounds like a complete cliché to say, but I've always been a Velvet Underground fan and the effect I want to have on people is the effect it has on me, looking at pictures of Lou Reed, John Cale and Sterling Morrison in 1966. The photographs of them in Andy Warhol's factory contain just about everything that made their music so awesome.
JIM REID, NOVEMBER 1985

Anybody who said to a record company, if they wanted to be signed, that they were influenced by The Velvet Underground, would be stupid. They're the last thing you'd want a record company to feel that they're dealing with, another Velvet Underground.
JOHN CALE, SEPTEMBER 1985

COCKLE
AND
SURE

-SHELL

And all along the desert shore
She wanders further evermore
While all her visions start to play
On the icicles of our decay.
KEVIN AYERS, 'DECADENCE', 1972

My music is not accidental. If you want it to be an accident, it is an accident, but it can also be something else. It can be very well thought out.
NICO, APRIL 1978

Future plans uncertain . . .
NME BOOK OF ROCK, 1977

I wonder where Nico is? I'd like to record with her again.
JOHN CALE, SEPTEMBER 1977

Possibly the only rumour about Nico that hasn't circulated so far is that she was once a man. Unlike Amanda Lear, Nico hardly needs such a drastic career boost. She is weird enough already.
MAUREEN PATON, *MELODY MAKER*, APRIL 1978

Listening to Nico is . . . essentially a cathartic ritual, best experienced with the shutters pulled tight and the gaslight casting eerie shadows on the wall.
DAVE THOMPSON, *MELODY MAKER*, AUGUST 1986

Actually, I am really Russian. I was born in Cologne, but my father and mother just happened to pass through. They were always travelling.
NICO, APRIL 1978

I have Turkish blood and Russian blood and German blood. I speak five languages. If I lived in Greece I could speak Greek, but I never lived there long enough. I know a few words. I know a Greek song, too, a very beautiful song. The title means, 'I was born to suffer'.
NICO, SEPTEMBER 1981

I am a pagan. But I am religious too. I guess religion also exists in a pagan, like pagan exists in religion, because it was there first.
NICO, APRIL 1978

I've been sort of disappearing and reappearing. I went to Los Angeles thinking I could sign a record contract. It may have been easier if I'd have been more patient about it. I left after two months.
NICO, JUNE 1978

I don't have a sense of time, time is timeless to me and I'm not in a hurry to get older. I mean, if I were worried about time, all the time, it would be terrible.
NICO, MAY 1981

I always put myself in a position where I am cornered. Why? I don't know, that is up to the psychoanalyst to say.
NICO, MAY 1981

I could be a grandmother soon. My son is 18 now.
NICO, MAY 1981

I know someone who always went to see the dinosaur in the Museum of Natural History, that was Donovan, a long time ago. He always went to see the dinosaur and made dates with his girlfriends underneath the dinosaur.
NICO, SEPTEMBER 1981

She might be pushing 50, but she still looks a debauched 30. Not for her the ravages of time. Perfectly preserved, she'll run forever, baffling 21st century anthropologists with her note-perfect impersonations of an industrial computer with a Greta Garbo fixation.
DAVE THOMAS, *MELODY MAKER*, JANUARY 1985

I find it so much fun to sing rock 'n' roll.
NICO, MAY 1981

Nico and Lou, they just entertain themselves and nobody else.
JOHN CALE, FEBRUARY 1983

A great lady. She's very together – for somebody who most people don't associate with being a professional musician. She's very determined, has a very professional attitude towards her work.
JOHN CALE, MAY 1985

I have a habit of leaving places at the wrong time, just when something big might have happened for me.
NICO, 1983

CHELSEA GIRL

They (MGM) originally wanted that to be a really MOR type album.
JOHN CALE, APRIL 1974

Jackson Browne, John Cale, Bob Dylan, they write beautiful songs. They are not easy to memorise, though.
NICO, MARCH 1975

It was a pity about the idiot who produced the album and put all those strings in.
LOU REED, JUNE 1977

'Wrap Your Troubles In Dreams', that's relentless. Lou's often said, 'Hey, some of these songs are just NOT WORTHY of human endeavour, these things are best left alone.' He may be right.
JOHN CALE, FEBRUARY 1983

Andy's film *Chelsea Girls* was about each Chelsea Girl Lou wrote about in the song. I was the one that I don't sing about. I only sing about the others.
NICO, MARCH 1975

If they just have allowed Cale to arrange it and let me do some more stuff on it . . . that song 'Chelsea Girl', everything on it, those strings, that flute, should have defeated it. But the lyrics, Nico's voice. It managed to somehow survive. We still got 'It Was A Pleasure Then', they couldn't stop us. We'd been doing a song like that in our beloved show, it didn't really have a title. Just all of us following the drone. And there it sits in the middle of that album.
LOU REED, JULY 1978

I was never happy with all the arrangements. I thought they were so bad. When I heard the album, when I heard what they'd done to it, I thought it wasn't right. It was very conventionally arranged.
NICO, MARCH 1975

THE MARBLE INDEX

The marble index of a mind forever, voyaging through strange seas of thought alone.
WILLIAM WORDSWORTH

I always combined his musical ability with the writing of my songs.
NICO, MARCH 1975

I had a toy piano on 'Evening Of Light', a piano for little children, and I started playing and we used that.
NICO, MARCH 1975

Before I did 'Marble Index' I didn't know I could arrange, but then I got lucky and found a very strong personality like Nico who threw me against the wall and I had to come and bounce back.
JOHN CALE, AUGUST 1975

It has to do with my going to Berlin in 1946 when I was a little girl and seeing the entire city destroyed. I like the fallen empire, the image of the fallen empire.
NICO, JUNE 1977

It's an artefact, not a commercial commodity. You can't sell suicide.
JOHN CALE, JUNE 1977

I did that just to prove to myself I could actually do something. It's really not very difficult working with Nico once you get her in the studio. She lays down a basic track with the harmonium and then you add the rest of the instruments.
JOHN CALE, APRIL 1974

I think 'Marble Index' could sell a large number of copies now. It makes more sense now.
NICO, MARCH 1975

I guess I'm always a little bit ahead. All the people dress the same way now as I was dressing on 'Marble Index'. Look at Spandau Ballet.
NICO, MAY 1981

DESERT SHORE

I have my own production company called Hit And Run Productions, to which Nico is signed. I want to put The English Chamber Orchestra behind her and write charts for them . . . and have less density and more depth. Density is what I think 'Marble Index' and 'Desert Shore' had.
JOHN CALE, 1971

'Marble Index' and 'Desert Shore' are beautiful albums but they're a little too intense. They're intense because they just have this one person playing all the instruments behind her . . . and it really gets a bit overbearing.
JOHN CALE, 1971

KEVIN AYERS

Nico is a woman you can only use for specific things, her voice and presence. I could certainly use her again, work with her on something. I don't know if she'd ever want to use me on anything, I doubt it. But making something together, an album, I don't think that's possible. We fight too much.
KEVIN AYERS, OCTOBER 1974

When I sang on that song, 'Irreversible Neural Damage', it was a misconception. I didn't like what they did to it. I don't think Kevin's happy with it. It should have been just straightforward, like two children singing together.
NICO, MARCH 1975

Kevin Ayers, whose June 1st 1974 show at The Rainbow introduced Nico and John Cale to British audiences for the first time in three years.

JUNE 1 1974 (I)

Kevin Ayers came back from the Rhone Valley to play the Rainbow, and decided to invite some guests to assist the festivities. He first invited his friend Nico, and through her contacted John Cale, another member of the original Velvet Underground. John, in London to record an album of his own, brought along Eno, who was greatly pleased to be working with some of his heroes (and heroine).

'JUNE 1, 1974' LP SLEEVE NOTES

I was going to do the concert at the Rainbow anyway, and initially it started out having a first act, a reggae group or something, and then me – or us – and we thought, 'Well, let's change the format a bit and try to turn it something better.' And then suddenly, uniquely, all these people were together. Nico was available which was quite uncommon. And Eno I'd met and talked to and liked . . . John Cale I didn't know much about but grew to like.

KEVIN AYERS, OCTOBER 1974

This is called 'Shouting In A Bucket Blues'. You should try it sometime. You put a bucket on your head and shout. I sound like Nico.

KEVIN AYERS, JUNE 1, 1974

An enchanted, estranged figure, Nico's performances are rare. At her last one in London (June 1, 1974) she outraged Teutonic sensibilities by singing the whole of 'Deutschland Uber Alles'.

OBSERVER, 1975

The encore, 'I've Got A Hard-On For You Baby', it was nice that everyone was joining in on the chorus with me. Even John Cale joined in. Nico tried to join in but suddenly realised that it wasn't her somehow.
KEVIN AYERS, OCTOBER 1974

It was an extraordinary concert, a rare pleasure for those who'd followed the performers' various careers through the past 10 years.
'JUNE 1, 1974' LP SLEEVE NOTES

THE END

The new Nico album I'm producing. Now that just drips.
JOHN CALE, NOVEMBER 1974

John Cale and Eno during the sessions for Nico's "The End" album in 1974.

Nico hasn't done it the way we (Lou and John Cale) are doing it. She'd just put it out. Those albums are so incredible, the most incredible albums ever made. 'The Marble Index', 'Desert Shore', 'The End' . . . you try to get a copy. You can't get 'em, you can't order them. They're in bins someplace. I have orders in five stores. They've disappeared off the face of the earth. Nico doing 'The End' is so unbelievable.
LOU REED, JANUARY 1976

I like the way 'Deutschland Uber Alles' is arranged, but I disagree with the way 'The End' is arranged. It wasn't my decision. I'm not responsible.
NICO, MARCH 1975

When I think about it I'm happy with all of it, apart from 'The End', and that's just another point of view, but it's a very obvious one.
NICO, MARCH 1975

I think Eno's playing is fantastic. But I think that's the way John saw it. He thinks my voice sounds very ancient, but I can't hear it. That album was recorded sincerely, but in the worst conditions of mind. The only thing that justifies it is that it is not pretentious or big-headed. It's very innocent.
NICO, MARCH 1975

She cried when it was finished. She did that with the others, too.
JOHN CALE, JUNE 1977

Jim Morrison – "We were spiritual brother and sister." (Nico)

JIM MORRISON

I want to record 'You're Lost Little Girl'. It all depends who is going to play for me. If it's The Doors, like I presume it'll be – they said they would do it – in that case I'll do it. But if it's not them, I won't do it I guess, because they can play exactly the way they were playing for Jim. That would be Jim. I wouldn't want a different variety.
NICO, JUNE 1978

Jim Morrison was my soul brother in a way. I still believe he's alive today because I'm his soul sister. That's why he's pretty much alive. That sounds very pretentious. But we have the same voices, almost. It just happens. We sing alike. It's natural.
NICO, APRIL 1978

DRAMA OF EXILE

I was dropped by Island because . . . I made a mistake. I said in *Melody Maker* to some interviewer that I didn't like negroes. That's all. They took it so personally . . . although it's a whole different race. I mean, Bob Marley doesn't resemble a negro, does he? He's an archetype of a Jamaican . . . but with the features like white people. I don't like the features. They're so much like animals . . . it's cannibals, no?
NICO, 1978

I've been disappearing. I've been disappearing from myself. I've become a total stranger to myself, and that's why I titled the record 'Drama Of Exile'. Because it's a drama being a stranger to yourself.
NICO, APRIL 1978

It was really boring, all that quiet stuff. And having been a member of The Velvet Underground rock 'n' roll is something I have to do at one point, even if only for one album. I want to combine it with Arabic music. I am part Turkish. Well, my father was part Turkish.
NICO, MAY 1981

I always wanted to sing 'Waiting For The Man' but Lou wouldn't let me. Lou was the boss and was very bossy. Anyway, I know a little bit more about the subject now than I did then. I find it something to occupy yourself with, running up and down the city.
NICO, MAY 1981

I recorded it as a tribute to Lou and because I wanted to sing rock 'n' roll. Because I'd never done it before and it's such a great rock 'n' roll song. I'm looking at it as a new song.
NICO, SEPTEMBER 1981

Apart from having so much choice I thought I could do one or two songs from Lou Reed's 'Berlin' album, but they're all so suicidal. 'Heroes' is not quite so destructive.
NICO, MAY 1981

'Sphinx' is dedicated to Andreas Baader because he had that hypnotic look, very hypnotic.
NICO, MAY 1981

I always like to write about people that are alive now, but that resemble those persons, heroes. I call them heroes, whether they are or not. Henry Hudson was a navigator.
NICO, SEPTEMBER 1981

I intend having a lyric sheet in this album. Cale and a few other people always thought that this would take away from the myth that was built around me if I put the lyrics on the sleeve.
NICO, SEPTEMBER 1981

'Orly Flight' is about a plane taking off for Madrid. I was waiting in the airport because the plane was leaving and I just started writing in the time at the airport. It's a nostalgic song, I guess. It's more for the airport than anything else – there's Charles DeGaulle airport now, which I don't like too much. It's too far away from Paris, and I like Orly.
NICO, SEPTEMBER 1981

CAMERA OBSCURA

It is not classic Nico (there's no 'Janitor Of Lunacy', 'Julius Caesar' or 'Genghis Khan') but hell, a Nico album's a Nico album and, accepting that John Cale's overwhelming presence should at least win him a co-billing in the credits, there really is no one else who could have made a record like this one.
DAVID THOMPSON, *MELODY MAKER*, AUGUST 1985

She's got a lot of depth in her personality that she didn't have before. Lyrics and sensibility. She's not as abrasive as she used to be.
JOHN CALE, SEPTEMBER 1985

MAUREEN TUCKER

She works for IBM now, and you can tell from us that she was perfect for the job. All we wanted was someone who could play on a telephone book.
LOU REED, JANUARY 1976

Lou, John and Nico at the Paris
Bataclan, June 1972.

You're getting a very straightforward interview, so relish it.
LOU REED, APRIL 1979

I hope somebody told you I don't like to answer personal questions.
LOU REED, JANUARY 1985

Lou Reed is a completely depraved pervert and pathetic death dwarf.
LESTER BANGS, *CREEM*, MARCH 1975

I'm amazed at just how different Lou and I were in our ideas now I've heard everything he's done since that time. It all sounds just like weak representations of tunes and nothing more. I mean some of his songs in The Velvets really made a point. Now he just appears to be going round in circles, singing about transvestites and the like. The only thing I've heard him do since, where he put up a good performance was on 'Sweet Jane'.
JOHN CALE, APRIL 1974

A close friend of mine always says that I bring out the idiocy in people, but I can also bring something out in them which is the best they've ever done. It's like with Nico and John Cale. They were fantastic with The Velvet Underground. They've done a lot of great things since. But they helped produce a great sound then.
LOU REED, JUNE 1977

People make music to express certain things or they write lyrics to express a certain thing and you can't talk about it because that was you talking. That was it.
LOU REED, APRIL 1979

I don't especially tell the truth most of the time anyway.
LOU REED, JULY 1973

Most people seem to think that if I didn't sit around writing stupid songs, there's nothing else I could do. But I went to acting school, and I can write prose. I'd write commercials.
LOU REED, JUNE 1977

Funniest thing on American television these days is the new commercial for Honda. Imagine the view: cameras tracking along the streets of New York, 'Walk On The Wild Side' playing on the soundtrack with the coloured girls going . . . you get the picture. Then in a final shot the camera sweeps along some boulevard and there's Lou Reed! Shades, leather, the works . . .
MELODY MAKER, JUNE 1985

Would you buy a used guitar from Peter Frampton?
LOU REED, MAY 1978

Really, both Iggy and Lou were just flamboyant closet cases fronting amateur hour wimp bands, the members of which would have been just as happy if they'd done acid drops and 'believed' in love and peace.
JULIE BURCHILL/TONY PARSONS, *THE BOY LOOKED AT JOHNNY*, 1978

When guys come in for autographs . . . They don't know what my real signature looks like 'cos I don't. I try different signatures all the time. So I say, why don't you sign it? And that always jams them. My new signature is like public school grade 5. I developed this style of handwriting about a year ago because I thought at this stage of the game it'd be nice to read whatever directions are left for myself such as 'Don't forget to lock yourself in the closet.'
LOU REED, MAY 1978

When he did eventually arrive he looked like his own grandmother.
PETE SILVERTON, MAY 1978

Jesus, he looks like an insect.
BUSBOY AT MAX'S, MARCH 1975

I admire Burt Reynolds a lot.
LOU REED, MARCH 1975

Lou Reed is a soft, selfish poet, committed to his art, his craft. Lou Reed wants to love himself. Lou Reed is his own biggest critic, and at the moment he's giving himself good reviews.
PAUL MORLEY, APRIL 1979

Did you know his real name is something like Finkelstein?
JOHN CALE, NOVEMBER 1977

I wish I'd written 'Sugar Sugar'.
LOU REED, JULY 1973

Why I've stuck with it is so I can make rock 'n' roll records. Because I make the records for myself.
The only criteria I have for a record is that I like it.
LOU REED, APRIL 1979

Lou has his whole life sorted out now. He's become the Jewish businessman we always
knew he was.
JOHN CALE, NOVEMBER 1977

When you buy a Lou Reed record you gotta expect a Lou Reed record. 'Metal Machine'
took care of that.
LOU REED, MAY 1978

I don't consider myself famous.
LOU REED, JANUARY 1985

I like Roxy Music, Bryan Ferry. I like David Bowie. That's it. Oh, I like disco as well.
LOU REED, APRIL 1979

Ou Reed – The Rock 'n' Roll Animal.

I love Lou but he has what must be a fragmented personality, so you're never too sure under any
conditions what you're going to have to deal with. Will he be boyishly charming, naïve – Lou is very
charming when he wants to be. Or will he be vicious – and if he is you have to figure out what's
stoking the fire. What drug is he on, or what mad diet? He had all sorts of strange dietary theories.
He'd eat nothing, live on wheat husks, I don't know. He was always trying to move mentally and
spiritually to some place where no one had ever gone before.
STERLING MORRISON, APRIL 1981

Since he got married he's been real happy, which makes me happy. Recently I dropped him a line
to say we'd had a new baby. I didn't expect a reply – I mean, what does he care? – but I got a very
sweet letter back.
MO TUCKER, MAY 1981

I just heard that Lou was gonna do a farewell-to-the-industry concert. Probably the first of many.
JOHN CALE, FEBRUARY 1983

Aaarrrgggh! Oooeeeoooh! Just releasing my tensions and inhibitions.
LOU REED, APRIL 1977

I wouldn't recommend me as entertainment. If I was going out I'm not the person I'd go see . . .
Then again, if I wanted to take a chance – I might.
LOU REED, MAY 1978

We don't keep in touch. He's turned into a regular home bird, settled down on a nice farm out in
Jersey. I don't see him. I don't even listen much to what he does.
JOHN CALE, FEBRUARY 1983

Just take a picture, I'm not doing any poses. I'm not a fucking orang-utan.
LOU REED, APRIL 1982

Lou, some part of him at least, really does like stability and the old cosy kitchen and homey living rooms. But if you'd seen some of his digs, they were depressing beyond all imagination. He had a place over in the East sixties. He was paying an outrageous amount of money for it so I thought I'd go over and see what this palace looked like. Well, you know how those high rise apartments are, they're real barren. And his was totally unfurnished, nothing there except some kind of pallet that he had pushed up against one corner. And a tape recorder and some old tapes and I guess a notebook, and an acoustic guitar. There was nothing in the fridge except a half-empty container of papaya juice; I mean nothing, not even vitamins. It was just the picture of isolation and despair.
STERLING MORRISON, APRIL 1981

I would like to live to a ripe old age and raise watermelons in Wyoming.
LOU REED, JULY 1973

Lou Reed, circa 1972.

You can always tell a bad Lou Reed song by the level of urgency he imparts it with.
CHRIS BOHN, *NEW MUSICAL EXPRESS*, APRIL 1983

Can I ask you something? Are you going to do a hatchet job on me?
LOU REED, APRIL 1979

I don't comment on past quotes.
LOU REED, JANUARY 1985

Lou was pretty coherent when I spoke to him on the phone two weeks ago. He told me about the Iron Crosses. He's always been like that, though – he was pretty crazed back when I first knew him. Maybe a little less crazed than now.
JOHN CALE, APRIL 1974

LOU REED – THE MUSIC

America's favourite cave dweller, Lou Reed, spent the summer in the studio with Richard Robinson putting finishing touches on his latest album.
CREEM, SEPTEMBER 1971

For that first album I spent a lot of time on the beach. You should have seen the original cover for that – me and my dog, with lots of seagulls in the background. I got so excited that they were going to take the photos that I had to take a valium. It wasn't used though.
LOU REED, JULY 1973

TRANSFORMER

A classic of mondo bendo rock.
LESTER BANGS, *CREEM*, JULY 1973

I don't think 'Transformer' is a decadent album. Singing about hustlers and gay people isn't decadent, is it? Singing about violence isn't decadent. The only song that I put in that category would be 'New York Telephone Conversation'.
LOU REED, JULY 1973

RCA had a lot of faith in Bowie. So they were willing to take a shot on another album, assuming he was going to be working with Lou. They made it clear that they were disappointed in Lou. They rejected the direction and specifically the production of the first album. But if David took over they could accept that.
DENNIS KATZ, 1981

The only motivation for 'Vicious' was that Warhol asked me to write a song called 'Vicious' – it would be so faaahbulous, y'know. So I said 'What kind of vicious', and he said, 'Oh, vicious, you hit me with a flower.' That's . . . outasight, y'know.
LOU REED, JULY 1973

'Transformer' is easily my best produced album. That has a lot to do with Mick Ronson. His influence was stronger than David's – but together as a team, they're terrific.
LOU REED, JULY 1973

What Mick and David did, it was very interesting. It's probably not what I would have done if they hadn't been around, but it was OK at the time.
LOU REED, JUNE 1977

That was me in drag on the back of 'Transformer'. No I'm lying. It's Ernie. We put a banana down his pants after being inspired by some gay pornographic magazines we picked up in Amsterdam.
LOU REED, JULY 1973

What about 'Perfect Day'? That's a lovely song – a description of a very straightforward affair.
LOU REED, JULY 1973

I may come out with a hard hat anti-gay song saying 'Get back in the closets, you fucking queers!' That'll really do it.
LOU REED, JULY 1973

DAVID BOWIE

In retrospect, I realised that the most significant aspect of my visit to Factory was my meeting with Lou Reed, and being given an acetate advance copy of The Velvet Underground's forthcoming album. That record was to play an important part in David's future.
KEN PITT, 1983

I met Lou at a party. Lou immediately started telling me about a guy who injected smack through his forehead. That's typical Lou. Up comes this funny, ragged, ragged little guy with broken teeth and Lou says, 'Don't talk to him, he's a junkie.' That was Iggy.
DAVID BOWIE, APRIL 1972

u and Bowie share a quiet moment
lowing Bowie's 1973 retirement.

David Bowie. He's a genius. He's brilliant.
LOU REED, JULY 1973

I would like to work with Bowie but he doesn't want to work with me. He hasn't said no yet, but I asked Brian Eno to ask him and he hasn't said anything yet.
NICO, APRIL 1978

Lou used to be a leader and proud. Now he's just a follower. Now he paints his fingernails – who needs David Bowie?
JOHN CALE, NOVEMBER 1974

I thought maybe I would do 'Look Back In Anger', but then I guess it's not such an important song as 'Heroes'. I had a few in mind to do, like 'Wild Is The Wind'. I sing that one just like Bowie.
NICO, MAY 1981

David's said a lot of nice things about me. He was in a bit of a mess the last time I saw him. I believe he's a bit more straightened out at the moment.
LOU REED, JUNE 1977

David is gaining and losing ground at the same time. He's managed to scuttle as much of one part of his audience as possible, and tried to go for another and they aren't there yet. I think he lacks people around him who might challenge him. He's in danger of becoming a guru.
LOU REED, MAY 1978

'Heroes' was written for me so I just felt like singing it. I know that as a fact. Because I was living in Berlin at the same time as Bowie was there. He recaptured my past, I guess. I can hear it from the lines 'Standing by the wall, the guns shot above our heads and we kissed.' That didn't happen of course, that was his fantasy. He had been chasing me for some time without result. And then when he was in Berlin he was kind of evading me because of what didn't happen before.
NICO, SEPTEMBER 1981

It's always much easier for them to say, 'David Bowie is really paranoid these days and he seems really drugged up, and gee, I wonder why.' Just because DeFries ripped him off, and his new lawyer, Lippman, after only two months is already doing it in the courts.
LOU REED, APRIL 1976

WALK ON THE WILD SIDE

Even Tony Blackburn played it – the poor, deluded fool!
ROY CARR/CHARLES SHAAR MURRAY, *DAVID BOWIE, AN ILLUSTRATED RECORD*, 1981

'Walk On The Wild Side' showed a lot of people where it's at. It has no moral stance. It's like all my songs. It's just an observation, a little movie, a little slice of something approaching reality.
LOU REED, JUNE 1977

My brother likes the one that goes, 'Shaved her legs and then he was a she.' My brother is eight.
LOU REED, JULY 1973

Warhol.

Hey, do you know, I heard it for the first time on the radio in Connecticut. They're trying to edit the song even more now, but at the end the DJ said, 'Hey, that's really funky, doo-bee-doo-bee-doo.'
LOU REED, JULY 1973

I thought they were going to claw my eyes out, but when I got back to New York, Candy Darling came up to me and said she's memorised all the songs, and that she wanted to make a Candy Darling – sings – Lou Reed album. That would be great. But it probably wouldn't sell more than a hundred copies.
LOU REED, JULY 1973

None of it's my personal life. They're people I know.
LOU REED, MAY 1973

I didn't like what 'Walk On The Wild Side' did. Or the way it was used. I was disgusted.
LOU REED, DECEMBER 1976

When we first came out, 'Heroin' was banned. They wouldn't even accept advertisements for it. And now 'Walk On The Wild Side' is Top 10.
LOU REED, MAY 1973

It's the culmination of a lot of things I always wanted to do. It's the most edited single that's probably ever been released. I mean, we did a slight edit and the radio stations have been editing the shit out of it. I mean, here all that's left are the do-do-doops. A lot of stations have edited out 'coloured girls' and 'valium'.
LOU REED, MAY 1973

TOURING WITH THE TOTS

His bass player is the ugliest person I have ever seen.
LESTER BANGS, *CREEM*, JULY 1973

He was an animal.
LOU REED, APRIL 1977

They just happened to be running around . . . which they probably still are, just laying there . . . except I'm sure they're no longer called The Tots. Benny was 17 . . . a good guitar player.
LOU REED, APRIL 1977

Warhol and Allen Ginsberg.

Who else but Lou Reed would get himself as fat as a pig, then hire the most cretinous band of teenage cortical cavities he could find to tote around the country on an all-time death drag tour?
LESTER BANGS, *CREEM*, MARCH 1975

ANDY'S CHEST

It's not often I shoot somebody. I didn't do it for nothing!
VALERIE SOLANIS, JUNE 1968

I don't understand some of the lines either. I just wrote them.
LOU REED, JULY 1973

GET BACK IN THE CLOSET YOU QUEERS

I got bored with wearing all that make-up. I actually played three gigs wearing it – pancake make-up, green lipstick, y'know. But I gave it up because it wasn't me. I'm the kind of person that would comment on that, but I'm not into make-up.
LOU REED, JULY 1973

I just think that everyone's into this scene because it's supposedly the thing to do right now. If they've got it in them, y'know, it won't necessarily involve make-up and all that, because just because you're gay doesn't mean you have to camp around in make-up.

That's just like platform shoes. You just can't fake being 'gay'. If they claim they're gay, they're going to have to make love in a gay style, and most of these people aren't capable of making that commitment. These kids can pretend to be as gay as can be, but when it comes down to it they just won't be able to make it. And that line – 'Everybody's bisexual' – that's a very popular thing to say right now. I think it's meaningless.
LOU REED, JULY 1973

The notion that everybody's bisexual is a very popular line now, but I think its validity is limited. I could say something like, if my album helps people decide who or what they are, then I will feel I have accomplished something in my life. But I don't feel that way at all. I don't think an album's gonna do anything. You can't listen to a record and say, 'Oh, that really turned me on to gay life, I'm gonna be gay.' A lot of people will have one or two experiences, and that'll be it. Things may not change one iota. It's beyond the control of a straight person to turn gay at the age he'll probably be listening to any of this stuff or reading about it.
LOU REED, JULY 1973

The make-up thing is just a style thing now, like platform shoes. If people have homosexuality in them it won't necessarily involve make-up in the first place. You can't fake being gay, because being gay means you're going to have to suck cock, or get fucked. I think there's a very basic thing in a guy if he's straight where he's just going to say no. 'I'll act gay, I'll do this and I'll do that, but I can't do that.' Just like a gay person if they wanted to act straight and everything, but if you said 'Okay, go ahead, go to bed with a girl', they're going to have to get an erection first.
LOU REED, JULY 1973

Being gay, I have found so many women – deluded creatures that they are – are attracted to you because you're not interested in them. Granted, I'm 'Lou Reed' and I have all this access, but even before I was 'Lou Reed' it happened that way. I could walk in and just because I wasn't interested, it came across as the ultimate cool – 'Hey, he really doesn't give a shit.' It never dawned on anybody that he doesn't give a shit because he couldn't.
LOU REED, MARCH 1979

I think women admire force all the more for not having it – nobody admires strength more than a weak person. It's axiomatic that a woman is all the more impressed that you could kill her. A straight guy might have something to learn from his gay friends, in that a woman can get turned off

if you're appreciative of her when what she really wants is to be smacked across the mouth.
LOU REED, MARCH 1979

My attitude often gets to be, 'Screw you, and I'll screw your girlfriends just for spite.' Which is a terrible way to do things because it's not like I would enjoy it. Of course they would, it goes without saying.
LOU REED, MARCH 1979

Joey Ramone and Lou Reed.

BERLIN

Throughout 'Berlin' the music is as black as his heart; a minimal texturing with little rhythm or melody, Lou's voice as despairingly flat as ever. The power of the music is almost cerebral, in the depth of the psychological insight it displays and the vividness of the portrait of two people helplessly crippling each other.
DAVID DOWNING, *FUTURE ROCK*, 1976

Blue Weaver is an asshole. Blue Weaver ought to . . . We didn't use what he did anyway. He doesn't know what he's talking about.
LOU REED, APRIL 1977

I love Bob Ezrin, by the way, that's probably one of the best albums ever, and Blue Weaver is an asshole. Like it was a total combination of everybody working really hard and combining their efforts, you don't divide it up into who did what . . . and he's a schmuck . . . a fucking ass.
LOU REED, APRIL 1977

I was coming off 'Transformer' and I'd had a hit single, but so that I wouldn't be bored I wanted to see whether I could have a hit single with a BAND rather than me on my own. So there was this big fight with RCA. I talked them into the veracity of the whole thing, of how astute it would be to follow up 'Walk On The Wild Side' with not just another hit single, but with a magnificent whatever. So I shoved it through. And the record sales, compared to 'Transformer', were a disaster for a normal person, but for me it was a total disaster. The record company did a quick scurry round like little bunnies, but I went somnambulant. It wasn't brain rot like some people think. I just kinda did no more.
LOU REED, DECEMBER 1976

'Berlin' was a song on the first Lou Reed album. It had been gestating obviously. That's why a little cocksucker like Blue Weaver ought to keep his fucking mouth shut . . . because he can't fucking play.
LOU REED, APRIL 1977

'Berlin' was REAL close to home. People would say, 'Lou – is that autobiographical?' And I'd say, 'Mmmmm, not bad.' Jesus, autobiographical? If only they KNEW! During the recording sessions, my old lady – who was a real asshole, but I needed a female asshole around to bolster me up, I needed a sycophant who I could bounce around and she fitted the bill . . . but she called it love, ha! – she tried to commit suicide in a bathtub in the hotel. Cut her wrists. She lived.
LOU REED, MAY 1978

Florian Schneider of Kraftwerk.

It was thought of as a concept right from the top. Right from the very beginning when Bobby and I worked it out. We just liked it . . . it was an adult album meant for adults . . . by adults for adults. And I think that's exactly what came out . . . Blue Weaver is an untalented son-of-a-bitch.
LOU REED, APRIL 1977

Before it came out *Rolling Stone* said it was going to be the 'Sergeant Pepper' of the seventies, and afterwards they wrote a pan and then they had a huge article criticising the pan. It won all kind of awards . . . it won the Thomas Edison award, and the best album of the year in *Stereo And Hi-Fi*. So critically it did not get panned, not in my book . . . not unless you look at some jerk-off magazine, a tit-and-ass magazine disguised as some junior hippy kind of thing. But outside of those morons – who are illiterate little savages anyway – it did really well.
LOU REED, APRIL 1977

Bob Ezrin is as bad as I am. He insists on doing things the hard way.
LOU REED, DECEMBER 1976

I think Lou Reed in his 'Berlin' is projecting the situation of a spy film, the spy standing in the fog smoking his cigarette.
FLORIAN, KRAFTWERK, SEPTEMBER 1975

'Berlin' was an album for adults. I want to make real albums. That whole thing started because I wanted to write real songs about something that was relevant.
LOU REED, DECEMBER 1976

If you wanna make adult rock records you gotta take care of all the people along the way. And it's not child's play. You're talking about managers, accountants, you're talking about the lowest level of human beings.
LOU REED, MAY 1978

'Berlin' was basically a movie in sound.
LOU REED, JUNE 1977

I'd love to see Polanski make a movie of 'Berlin'. Little devil!
LOU REED, APRIL 1979

'Berlin' is a very good album that more than holds its own. It's very potent, just as powerful just as magical an experience. It has a depth and perspicacity that is just exquisite today.
LOU REED, APRIL 1977

A gargantuan slab of maggoty rancour that may well be the most depressed album ever made.
LESTER BANGS, *CREEM*, MARCH 1975

As a matter of fact, Blue Weaver should . . .
LOU REED, APRIL 1977

It was great what Bobby (Ezrin) did. If I was in charge I would have done it somewhat differently. But he did a great job, everybody on that album did a great job. I still think it's a fantastic album.
LOU REED, JANUARY 1976

ROCK 'N' ROLL ANIMAL

I'm not being a martyr or any of that shit, but I had to get popular. People love that album. I know why they do. Prakash John) is a good bass player. (Steve) Hunter and Dick Wagner are with Alice now. People always used to say the band overshadows Reed. I picked the bloody band! In 'Oh Jim' that guitar duel that goes on is fantastic, so classic, and the only reason it goes on is because I get off on it. Hunter/Wagner, that was for real on stage.
LOU REED, JANUARY 1976

RCA put out 'Rock 'n' Roll Animal' and it was like a walking time-warp to me. It has a perfect sound, though. Because I mixed it. The engineer just left. He didn't know how to record it. I couldn't stand what they were doing. Cleaning it up! And I went, 'Oh No!' and there was another big fight.
LOU REED, DECEMBER 1976

Lou ended up doing album after album of reissues of the same song. 'Rock 'n' Roll Animal' is only worth it to me because of Dick Wagner's guitar playing.
JOHN CALE, FEBRUARY 1983

I wanted to get The Velvets' stuff known. That's what I was doing. Like the 'Heroin' that got popular on the album. It's just desecrated. It's so blasphemous it's horrifying. I understand why people like it, but it almost killed me. It was so awful.
LOU REED, JANUARY 1976

It's . . . greugh . . . like . . . ARGH! . . . having a Black and Decker stuck up yer nose and . . . MWAAAUK!! . . . a tractor . . . BRAAA!!! park on your head . . . and . . . YAAAA!!! a herd of rhinos . . . NGLOOOOOORT!!!!
GIOVANNI DADOMA, *SOUNDS*, MAY 1977

SALLY CAN'T DANCE

'Kill Your Sons'. That's really an old song of his.
JOHN CALE, APRIL 1974)

Speaking of gastric disorders, I used to really despise 'Sally Can't Dance'. Remember how the press ads had this line that said, 'Your mother wouldn't like it' and the old brain cells immediately produced the reply, 'Course not, she's not dumb!'
GIOVANNI DADOMO, *SOUNDS*, MAY 1977

It was produced in the slimiest way possible. I like leakage. I wish all the Dolbys were just ripped outa the studio. I like the old Velvets records. I don't like Lou Reed records.
LOU REED, FEBRUARY 1976

'Sally Can't Dance' . . . With all the junk in there, it's still Lou Reed. I sound terrible, but I was singing about the worst shit in the world.
LOU REED, MAY 1978

Lou, waiting to see why Sally can't dance.

'Animal Language' isn't obvious. Who do you think the animals are? You think it's a dog and cat?
LOU REED, MARCH 1975

'Sally Can't Dance' is cheap and tedious.
LOU REED, FEBRUARY 1976

It went Top 10. What a horror. It goes to number 10 and it sucks.
LOU REED, JANUARY 1976

I slept through 'Sally Can't Dance', that's no big secret. They'd make a suggestion and I'd say,
'Oh, all right.' I'd do the vocals in one take, in about 20 minutes, and then it was 'goodbye'. But the
worse the albums were, the more they'd sell.
LOU REED, DECEMBER 1976

LOU REED LIVE

I dunno about Lou Reed being the Sinatra of the seventies. Personally, I feel that under the
circumstances, Judy Garland would be a far more appropriate comparison.
ROY CARR, *NME*, MARCH 1975

METAL MACHINE MUSIC

It is the only recorded work I know of seriously done as well as possible as a gift, if one could
call it that, from a part of a certain head, to a few others. Most of you won't like this, and I
don't blame you at all.
LOU REED, LINER NOTES TO 'METAL MACHINE MUSIC', 1976

The greatest album ever made.
LESTER BANGS, *CREEM*, MARCH 1976

Recommended cuts – none.
BILLBOARD, MARCH 1976

Just imagine that wired little weasel, marching through the offices of one of the biggest media
conglomerates in the world with his machine tapes in his hand, not just confident but downright
cocky that what he had here was the greatest masterpiece in musical history. Lou took 'Metal
Machine Music' straight to the top, to Kenneth Glancy, President of RCA Records, and worked
his way down from there. Office to office and every one he goes into he just presses the
button and out comes ZZZZZZZRRRRRRRRREEEEEEEEEGGGGGGGGGGGRRRRRAAAAA
RRRRRRRRGGGGGGGGGGGHHHHHHNNNNNNNNNNNNIIIIIIIIIIEEEEEEEEERRRRRRRRRRRRR
RR.
LESTER BANGS, *CREEM*, FEBRUARY 1976

My ultimate guitar solo . . . *The* ultimate guitar solo.
LOU REED, APRIL 1983

I first started thinking about 'Metal Machine Music' as far back as when John used to work with LaMonte Young. It took a long, long time. It's way more complex than people realise, but that's all right. I wasn't going to put it out even, I made it for myself. John and I were always making tapes. A lot are still circulating around. We made soundtracks for underground movies of the time. We always encouraged bringing tape recorders to our jobs.
LOU REED, JANUARY 1976

I've got something here that is the stuff I wanted to do, that I meant by heavy metal. I had to wait a couple of years so I could get the equipment, now I've got it and it's done. I could have sold it as electronic classical music, except the one I've got that I've finished now is heavy metal, no kidding around.
LOU REED, MARCH 1975

It was all purposive and very highly calculated. I put a cover on it like 'Rock 'n' Roll Animal', so that it looked like a live rock 'n' roll album.
LOU REED, APRIL 1977

There's some frequencies on there that are dangerous. What I'm talking about is like in France, they have a sound gun. It's a weapon. It puts out frequencies which kill people. They've had this weapon since 1945. Maybe that's why they play such bad rock 'n' roll.
LOU REED, FEBRUARY 1976

'Metal Machine Music' is probably one of the best things I ever did, and I've been thinking about doing it ever since I've been listening to LaMonte. I had also been listening to Xenakis a lot. You know the drone thing? Well, doing it with a band you always had to depend on other people. And inevitably you find that one person is stronger than another.
LOU REED, FEBRUARY 1976

You don't listen to it on speakers because if you do you miss half the fun.
LOU REED, FEBRUARY 1976

My pet hermit crab, Spud, who sometimes goes for days at a time curled up inside his shell in a corner of the cage so you gotta check if he's dead, likes 'MMM' a lot. Every time I put it on, he comes out of his shell and starts crawling happily around the sand and climbing the bars. It is, in fact, the only time I ever see him get any exercise. Either that or he's dancing.
LESTER BANGS, *CREEM*, MARCH 1976

It was marketed wrong. There was an information breakdown. They wanted to put it out on Red Seal, and I said no, because that would be pretentious. I wasn't going to put it out at all. But a friend of mine at another record company asked to hear it, and said why don't you play it for the head of classical music at RCA. I think 'Metal Machine' got him fired. I played it for him and he loved it. I thought he must be mad, but he said we really must put it out.
LOU REED, FEBRUARY 1976

I'm not going to apologise to anybody for 'Metal Machine Music'. And I don't think any disclaimer should have been put on the cover. Just because some kid paid $7.98 for it. I don't care if they paid $59.98 or $75 for it, they should be grateful I put the fucking thing out, and if they don't like it they should go eat ratshit.
LOU REED, FEBRUARY 1976

Why do people go and see movies like *Jaws, The Exorcist* and *Ilsa, She-Wolf Of The SS*? So they can get beaten over the head with baseball bats, have their nerves wrenched while electrodes are being stapled to their spines and be generally brutalised at least once every 15 minutes or so . . . Here there's no 15 minutes of bullshit padding between brutalisations. Anybody who got off on *The Exorcist* should like this record.
LESTER BANGS, *CREEM*, MARCH 1976

I don't like any of my albums except 'Metal Machine Music'. I use it to go to sleep sometimes. Why don't I like the others? Because they're not 'Metal Machine'.
LOU REED, APRIL 1977

I profess total and complete ignorance.
ERNIE GILBERT, RED SEAL A&R DIRECTOR, FEBRUARY 1976

It was a giant 'Fuck You'.
LOU REED, FEBRUARY 1976

CONEY ISLAND BABY

People who think I got something out of 'Metal Machine', monetarily or otherwise, should have another think coming. All it accomplished was negative. It'll be that much harder for 'Coney Island Baby' to prove itself. A lot of people got turned off and I am so happy to lose the people who got turned off. You have no idea. It just clears the air. That's the end of it. If anybody wanted 'Coney Island Baby' it was going to be my way.
LOU REED, JANUARY 1976

They're not what people think of as archetypal Lou Reed songs, but they forgot on the first Velvets' album, 'I'll Be Your Mirror', 'Femme Fatale'. I've always liked that kind of stuff and now you're going to have a whole album full of it. 'The Many Moods Of Lou Reed', just like Johnny Mathis, and if they don't like it they can shove it.
LOU REED, FEBRUARY 1976

I didn't sleep through this one. I could play this for people and really be proud of it. I was never that much interested in the other albums. I mean, they're OK, but they're not Lou Reed albumş. Or if they were, I was on automatic pilot. But this one is the way we all wanted it. If people don't like it, they're not liking my kind of album.
LOU REED, JANUARY 1976

Everybody connected with 'Coney Island Baby' knows that to have me record it, it couldn't be tampered with. There's no outside disruptive forces, no advice, no looking over my shoulder.
LOU REED, JANUARY 1976

I made 'Coney Island Baby' and was served three times with three separate subpoenas, one before, one during and one after. OK, two injunctions they Lou's former management) tried to get against it. It was just two weeks ago that the last injunction against it was denied. If it had not been denied the record would have been recalled.
LOU REED, APRIL 1976

'Coney Island Baby' is me from top to bottom. And if you don't like it, stuff it.
LOU REED, APRIL 1976

ROCK 'N' ROLL HEART

His new album reveals that if he is still the Prince of Decadence, then he is the spirit of rock 'n' roll's Guardian Angel as well.
CAROLINE COON, *MELODY MAKER*, DECEMBER 1976

My records are for real. But that song 'I Believe In Love' – coming from Lou Reed that is supposed to be a very strange statement.
LOU REED, DECEMBER 1976

I still don't know the lyrics to 'Rock 'n' Roll Heart'. I make them up as I go along.
LOU REED, DECEMBER 1976

I had a couple of songs before we went into the studio, but they changed. The rest I wrote in the studio. It's much more fun that way. No, it isn't expensive because I'm very quick. It took 27 days to record that album, including mixing. It took as long to mix as it did to record.
LOU REED, DECEMBER 1976

'Rock 'n' Roll Heart' is very well produced.
LOU REED, DECEMBER 1976

'Rock 'n' Roll Heart' is in tune. Perfect. Funny.
LOU REED, DECEMBER 1976

I've got another guitar player. His name is Geoffrey. Just Geoffrey. If he doesn't work out, I don't want people to know his last name.
LOU REED, APRIL 1977

One kid said to me he really liked the lyrics on 'Banging On My Drum'. And I said, 'But there are no lyrics' and he said 'FRUSTRATION'. I thought I'd written a song about having lots of fun, fun, fun . . . But apparently not. *Rolling Stone* said that song was all about masturbation, so that just goes to show.
LOU REED, DECEMBER 1976

It's very hard to find someone who can play dumb on a nice rock 'n' roll song. But I can play really dumb piano. And I write songs with only two chords in them. Like 'Banging On My Drum'.
LOU REED, DECEMBER 1976

STREET HASSLE

Nobody wants to be a rhythm guitarist any more except niggers. You know that Marvin Gaye song 'Gotta Give It Up', the album version, that rhythm guitarist, his throwaways are riffs

that people would give their left ball for. I tried to do that kind of guitar on 'I Wanna Be Black'. Naturally I fucked it up.
LOU REED, JULY 1978

'Street Hassle' is that serious. It's me on the line. And I'm talking to them one to one. It gets very intense . . . It's scary 'cos it looks like I'm making myself so vulnerable.
LOU REED, MAY 1978

'I Wanna Be Black' . . . it was transmogrified – that's a big word meaning Catholicism. You want to know the real Lou Reed? Turn around. Now bend over.
LOU REED, FEBRUARY 1979

'Street Hassle', the masterpiece. People are always using whole string sections. We just zeroed in on the groovy part.
LOU REED, JULY 1978

'Street Hassle' was recorded live in Germany. They didn't understand a word of English – like most of my audience. They're fucked up, assholes, what difference does it make? Can they count from one to 10?
LOU REED, FEBRUARY 1979

'Street Hassle' is the best album I've done. 'Coney Island Baby' was a good one, but I was under siege. 'Berlin' was 'Berlin', 'Rock 'n' Roll Heart' is good compared to the rest of the shit that's going around. As opposed to 'Street Hassle' they're all babies.
LOU REED, MAY 1978

The best thing to do with this album is blink your eyes and think of this as Lou Reed's first solo album since he left The Velvets and the whole thing will hit a clear cut and precise perspective in your head. 'Street Hassle' is as perfect an album as you'll ever want to hear.
JOE FERNBACHER, *CREEM*, JUNE 1978

BRUCE SPRINGSTEEN

He was in the studio below, and for that little passage I'd written (in 'Street Hassle') I thought he'd be just perfect, 'cos I tend to screw those things up. Like 'I Found A Reason', it is my best recitation, but I just couldn't resist that 'Walking hand in hand with myself' part. I'm too much of a smart ass. But I knew Bruce would do it seriously, 'cos he really is of the street.
LOU REED, JULY 1978

TAKE NO PRISONERS

It presents a portrait of Lou Reed more authentic and vivid than any documentary or any amount of interviews could possibly achieve, and exploits more fully than on any previous recording the full impact of his often pathologically cruel – but incessantly hilarious – humour.
ALLAN JONES, *MELODY MAKER*, DECEMBER 1978

Everybody said I never talked. I was in my home town of New York, so I talked. I even thought of titling it 'Lou Reed Talks And Talks And Talks' but we called it 'Take No Prisoners' because we were doing a job, a quite phenomenal booking in a tiny hotel in Quebec, where they'd normally have a little dance-band. I dunno what we were doing there, but . . . All of a sudden this drunk guy sitting alone at the front shouts, 'LOU! MAN! TAKE NO PRIS'NERS, LOU!' and then he took his head and smashed it as hard as he could to the drumbeat. We saw him doing it and we were taking bets that that man would never move again. But he got up and BAM BAM on the table! And that was only halfway through. What was gonna be the encore? He mighta cut his arm off!
LOU REED, APRIL 1978

I wanted to have a live album that was something I would have liked. There'd been previous live albums, but I hadn't liked them. I thought I was the minority stock holder.
LOU REED, FEBRUARY 1979

It is a comedy album. Lou Reed talks and talks and talks. Lou Reed, songwriter, is dried up – ran out of inspiration.
LOU REED, FEBRUARY 1979

THE BELLS

This is what you'd call an impressive failure. There were a few traps here, seemingly unwittingly laid, a few monolithic mud pies that the mind is not encouraged to slide through so that after several listenings one tends to avoid certain cuts.
RICHARD C. WALLIS, *CREEM*, AUGUST 1979

I already wrote some of the songs with Nils Lofgren. We got together with Bob Ezrin, and wrote some really good things together. It's going to be a big sound, various machines making the guitar sound like a symphony. It will be so grand.
LOU REED, MARCH 1979

It would seem that Reed's gifts of vision and expression are fully revivified and newly honed to a lethal edge.
ROLLING STONE, APRIL 1979

It sounds like no other Lou Reed album.
ARISTA PRESS RELEASE, MAY 1979

It's about a suicide. Not a bad suicide, but an ecstatic movement. It's a guy who's in love with Broadway or whatever, and he's on the edge of the building and he looks out and he thinks he sees a brook and he says there are the bells, thinks he sees the bells and as he points he tumbles over a drum roll. It's beautiful. It's not negative, it's here comes the bells.
LOU REED, APRIL 1979

On this album I hadn't realised it but I haven't co-written songs with anybody since The Velvet Underground. But on this album, every song is co-written. A guy called Nils Lofgren is on it. Well, three of the songs I wrote with him.
LOU REED, APRIL 1979

(MUSIC FROM) THE ELDER

(*In 1979 Lou was called in, at the suggestion of producer Bob Ezrin, to contribute lyrics to the new Kiss concept album*).

Lou Reed was so into the project, when we called him and explained it over the phone to him he said, 'I'll get back to you in an hour.' And he called back an hour later with good basic lyrics to 'Mr Blackwell', 'World Without Heroes' and a lot of other stuff that hasn't been used yet.
PAUL STANLEY, KISS, 1980

THE BLUE MASK

The sleeve is the same as 'Transformer'. It is the same picture. Unfortunately, your cover is different to the one in the United States. There, when you move the picture under the light it changes from the 'Transformer' face to the mask and back, like those buttons you see people wearing. I was amazed to find that it didn't do that over here. It was supposed to be like a mask over that whole period of time.
LOU REED, APRIL 1982

There are no overdubs. Everything was done live in the studio except the vocals.
LOU REED, APRIL 1982

I don't get into philosophy or moralising or anything I consider pretentious, like telling you what to do or telling you what I think. I never tell you what to think, I always tell you a little story. It's not always my story. So I don't know how much to tell you 'My House' is all me. 'The Gun' is none of me. 'The Gun' is as opposite as you can get. The guy in 'The Gun' is a vicious, stupid, mean so-and-so. But I know people like that and I wanted to act it out for you people who might not know someone like that, so you can see what it's like.
LOU REED, APRIL 1982

My new album is like a Velvet Underground record.
LOU REED, APRIL 1982

LEGENDARY HEARTS

There's supposed to be this tension between . . . Now this sounds awfully pretentious when we start talking this way, but anyway, it's about the desire to possess something that may not be possessable. It's also the problem of desire and fantasy against the reality, and what happens when the two meet each other in the alley. Or in the armchair for that matter.
LOU REED, APRIL 1983

NEW SENSATIONS

It's user-friendly.
LOU REED, AUGUST 1984

'New Sensations' is vastly different in sounds and ideas from my other records. There's drum machines on this one because I discovered they were the key to the sound I was after. Luckily, my drummer, Fred Mahler, really loves drum machines so he and the engineer spend days programming the different patterns. I also recorded with a click track for the first time. Ten years ago if you'd punched up a click track I'd have walked out, but now I can see they're useful in keeping time and letting you worry about where to put the feeling rather than always listening out for the drums.
LOU REED, AUGUST 1984

I wanted to have fun with it. And there were certain sounds that I heard on the radio – a certain kind of bass and drums thing, for instance, that were really strong and exciting, and I wanted to have that.
LOU REED, JANUARY 1985

In many ways it's like an early Velvet Underground album because I played all the guitar parts on 'New Sensations' and in the early Velvet Underground I generally told people exactly hat they should be playing.
LOU REED, AUGUST 1984

I always like my most recent album best, and that applies to every single one of them. I'm always most excited about the last one when I get out of the studio, and then, having heard it so much I'll suddenly get very sick of it and won't listen to it for a year.
LOU REED, JANUARY 1985

LESTER BANGS

If he ever started writing good things about me it'd be the kiss of death.
LOU REED, SEPTEMBER 1975

With a name like that . . . good Lord! I can't help it if someone like that idolises me . . . it's not my fault. If someone idolises you that much it embarrasses them . . . they read some kind of sexual overtones into it and they're embarrassed. So they have to criticise the work, rather than just look into it and realise that they're just fucking insects. Lester's embarrassed by the fact that he's an insect. I'm not embarrassed by the fact that Lester's an insect . . . insects are drawn by shining lights, by stars. So of course he's drawn to me.
LOU REED, APRIL 1977

The best way to get anything publicised is to tell Lester, 'Please don't print that.' And he'll print it. The very best way is to let him overhear something accidentally on purpose.
LOU REED, SEPTEMBER 1975

Oh please . . . what little scumbag would say something like that?
LOU REED, APRIL 1977

You really are an asshole, Lester. You went past assholism into some kinda urinary tract.
LOU REED, MARCH 1975

He's really an insect, because . . . he should be writing about sports. He should get out of rock 'n' roll because he's just a big schlub from Detroit. He's fat and he's got a moustache. How would you like to have someone like that worshipping you, and if you sneeze in the morning he'll catch cold?
LOU REED, APRIL 1977

I never met a hero I didn't like. But then, I never met a hero.
LESTER BANGS, *CREEM*, MARCH 1975

I wouldn't shit in Lester's nose.
LOU REED, APRIL 1977

Lou and Nico at the Paris Bataclan, January 1972.

JOHN CALE

I'm bent on proving that you can make a living as a musician and not die young and crazy like Mozart.
JOHN CALE, APRIL 1981

John Cale, who was as brilliant as Lou Reed, has been more consistent (than Lou), but throughout his solo career he has not simply avoided success, but tried to throttle it with both hands.
MARY HARON, *NEW MUSICAL EXPRESS*, APRIL 1981

Phil Spector had a good idea. He took rhythm and blues and gave it a Wagnerian background. I like breaking things down into the lowest common denominator and seeing how much tension can be created between the individual parts, in order to create a loud noise.
JOHN CALE, APRIL 1981

Cale's incredible, everybody knows that. Sure. I mean, one of the things I want to do, and I know John does too, is to get together. He's getting his solo stuff out of the way, he's getting popular. And he really should. But just like the stuff I'm doing, people don't know what we can really do. What he's putting out now is not a *nth* of what he can do. The thing is, if he puts it out now, it's too much of a different direction. That'd be the end of it.
LOU REED, JANUARY 1976

A cult figure is a guy who hasn't got the musical ability to make the charts.
JOHN CALE, MAY 1975

The man's obviously a ghost.
MICK GOLD, *CREEM*, OCTOBER 1974

It's beginning to dawn on me that not many people are convinced of my commercial appeal.
JOHN CALE, AUGUST 1980

'Ere, is that really JJ Cale?
LONDON RECORDING ENGINEER, APRIL 1974

IGGY AND THE STOOGES

I remember Iggy as this incredibly skinny kid who just used to drink beer – his apartment was piled up with beer cans and the remains of old pizzas. You know he taught his band exactly how to play their instruments, don't you? Also, when he played live all these girls would go absolutely bananas. Sometimes he'd take 'em under the stage for 10 seconds and then pull them out and get back on stage while they'd be trying to drag him back to finish it off.
JOHN CALE, APRIL 1974

I used to be real naïve. Thanks to Nico I got corrupt. I am totally into corruption.
IGGY POP, 1977

Iggy is stupid. Very sweet but very stupid. He's not even a good imitation of a bad Jim Morrison, and *he* was never any good anyway.
LOU REED, MARCH 1975

Iggy and The Stooges were great. Very light . . . they were doing a hard and straight rock 'n' roll but the eventual effect was very light. Iggy had a lot of innocence. He'd walk out to the edge of the audience and fall into the audience. He'd pick up a table and threaten them, then turn round and hug the table. It was a beneficent attitude. He wasn't into cutting himself with bottles and the like.
JOHN CALE, JUNE 1977

Iggy was just normal. He certainly wasn't unhappy. I just took the band into the studio and we did it as quickly as I would do anything with a young punk band today.
JOHN CALE, NOVEMBER 1977

CHURCH OF ANTHRAX

That was recorded before 'Vintage Violence' and it was all improvising. I had Bobby Columby (of Blood Sweat And Tears) and Bobby Gregg on drums and Terry (Riley) overdubbed a whole mess of stuff and I went in to mix it. After I was finished, Terry walked in, heard the mix, turned around and walked out. He felt somewhat dispossessed of his personality on the record.
JOHN CALE, APRIL 1981

You can't dance to 'Church Of Anthrax'.
GIOVANNI DADOMO, *SOUNDS*, JUNE 1977

VINTAGE VIOLENCE

Basically it was an exercise to see if I could write tunes.
JOHN CALE, APRIL 1974

There's not too much originality on 'Vintage Violence'. It's just someone teaching himself to do something. I was trying to see if I could write songs. I'd never done it before.
JOHN CALE, MAY 1975

I was masked on 'Vintage Violence'. I didn't realise at the time, but the cover tells you that. You're not really seeing the personality.
JOHN CALE, OCTOBER 1974

Iggy Pop: five years before Bowie latched onto him, Cale and Nico had already pinpointed his talents.

The *modus operandi* of all the records from 'Vintage Violence' onwards was a continuation of The Velvets – we could improvise songs on-stage, nothing would have anything in common with the previous one, we could record each performance and have them all representative of states of mind.
JOHN CALE, OCTOBER 1985

THE ACADEMY IN PERIL

After what happened with 'Vintage Violence' and 'Church Of Anthrax' I figured that I wouldn't mess around with rock 'n' roll any more, that I would do a straight classical music thing. And then the first thing I did when I went into the studio was put down a song called 'King Harry'. That's sort of reggae – I love that music. Anyway, there is rock 'n' roll on my album, but I don't know where it stands. It has three rock 'n' roll pieces – 'King Harry', 'Days Of Steam' and 'The Philosopher'. Ron Wood played slide guitar on 'The Philosopher'.
JOHN CALE, 1971

Andy Warhol, Nico and John Cale.

The three orchestral pieces, 'John Milton', 'Captain Morgan's Lament' and 'The Balance' just didn't hang together interestingly enough to be a symphony. And those titles fit better than a collective title, so I just left them as they were. At first it bothered me that it was all so Elizabethan, but then I decided to make it more Elizabethan. But I'm really encouraged now because I'm going to go and think carefully about a symphony. I have to spend time at it, not go into the studio and say, 'Well, we'll start here and see what happens.'
JOHN CALE, 1971

I'm glad I got down to writing orchestral music, which is something I've wanted to do for a long time. And I was really glad that I remembered all the tricks they taught me in school about how to write for the orchestra.
JOHN CALE, 1971

The Academy in Pearl Harbour.
JOHN CALE, 1975

Andy Warhol did the cover and it's got a lot of holes in the front. And through the holes you can see my eyes . . . close-up of one eye at a time. Some are squinting, some are irreverent. He's very clever. He did one for me before, for 'Vintage Violence', that I never got to use . . . It was really great. The reason I didn't use it was because he showed me with long hair and I didn't look like that any more.
JOHN CALE, 1971

It was a straight swap. Andy used 'Days Of Steam' for the soundtrack of 'Heat' and gave me the artwork for 'Academy'.
JOHN CALE, APRIL 1974

I feel that I really dived into this album and tried to approach it the same way I approached the Nico albums – with a lot of overdubbing. I spent a week at the Manor in England recording and after that I had the bare essentials of some pieces that I wrote down. But the idea that I could do a symphony the same way that I could do a Nico album just isn't true. The music was sort of written in my head – improvising – and then I copied down what I heard and orchestrated it. When the orchestra, with the 85-piece string section, played the music, a lot of it sounded entirely different than what I originally thought would happen.
JOHN CALE, 1971

I doubt whether it will sell many copies, but I'm glad I did it because it encouraged me to do more. The next time I've got to do songs, I've got a lot of songs to put on it, but I don't want to do all my own songs necessarily. I just listened to Benjamin Britten's 'Serenade For Tenor Horn And Strings' – and there are a couple of things in there, like the dirge and the first piece in there are really nice.
JOHN CALE, 1971

I had to wait around for two weeks for The Royal Philharmonic, but I was pleased with the results. I had forgotten what it was like to work with musicians like that, they really need an authoritative figure.
JOHN CALE, 1971

It took three weeks in England to do this one and it wasn't enough. It was really painful getting that done in three weeks. I never used to think about that because I figured that you take your chances and you go with what you've got. But now I've got to make room for some leeway, and start and do three tracks and then think about it for three months and then do another three tracks but not just go bang bang bang, because all you eventually get is a representation of yourself on the days that you did it. For those three weeks that's where you are. And the more time you give yourself, you can relax a bit and think about it and you're not so tense and things come out that you didn't know were there, you have time to peruse what you do.
JOHN CALE, 1971

'Academy In Peril' is a paltry excuse . . . There are a few moments there that are worthwhile. But it's wishy-washy Vaughan Williams stuff.
JOHN CALE, OCTOBER 1985

JONATHAN RICHMAN AND THE MODERN LOVERS

The Modern Lovers' significance is usually considered to be their carrying on a tradition begun by The Velvet Underground and continued by The Stooges. The Modern Lovers kept this tradition going, added to it and eventually handed it over to what became the New Wave.
BILL FLANAGAN, *TROUSER PRESS*, NOVEMBER 1979

We were having a party and Jonathan wandered in with all these people who had acted in Andy Warhol movies. He had the new Velvet Underground album, 'Loaded' which I had not heard and he was very excited by it. He put it on and sort of danced in our kitchen singing about it.
JERRY HARRISON, NOVEMBER 1979

Jonathan Richman: Warner Brothers scrapped the tapes of his 1973 collaboration with John Cale because of the vinyl shortage.

Jonathan used to hang around Velvet Underground rehearsals and sleep on Lou Reed's sofa.
ERNIE BROOKS, NOVEMBER 1979

I met all of them back then, when they used to play Boston. I would watch them rehearse. I would watch them almost every time they came. I saw them do about 100 live shows, anyway, plus rehearsal time. I watched them for hours rehearsing. I would watch them work out songs. I was a kid hanging out, and an obnoxious one at that. I took loads of pictures, I've got tons of pictures of them, I even made a movie that I gave to someone, you can't see anything in it, but a little colour movie of them rehearsing. I can tell you loads about the early Velvets if you ever wanted to hear. Jonathan tells most.
JONATHAN RICHMAN, SEPTEMBER 1977

The latest thing Jonathan wanted to do is to go on the stage and masturbate in front of the audience. He's very weird – the rest of the group goes on dancing and he stays in his room. He doesn't go out with girls. Right now they're not doing anything, though, hanging round Boston. Last thing I heard Jonathan was trying to bring in five new members whose only function would be to hit newspapers on their hands in time to the music.
JOHN CALE, APRIL 1974

PARIS 1919

It has a blend of classical and rock 'n' roll that's indeterminate. 'Paris' is a warm, listener's album, not a songwriter's album.
JOHN CALE, FEBRUARY 1983

The first track we did, 'A Child's Christmas In Wales' was the most straightforward, and we didn't do an awful lot to it, so although it fits into the album very well, some of the others were a bit more interesting to work on. On 'Hanky Panky Nohow' we did all that ourselves just one night. Somebody had recently died and we heard the news on the night we were recording that track, and on each song, there's always a strange atmosphere. Something started to develop, and that was just John and I playing on the track, just overdubbing viola.
CHRIS THOMAS, 1982

I think the album with John Cale was a direct result of (my working on) the Procol Harum live album. I think he heard the album and liked it. I didn't know quite what to expect from John, although I used to like The Velvet Underground. But . . . he's a pretty fascinating character.
CHRIS THOMAS, 1982

There were glimmers of light on 'Paris'. It was beginning to come through the cracks. That album's all right, but I don't want to make Procol Harum albums all my life.
JOHN CALE, OCTOBER 1974

Germany had some art gallery series where one side of the record was 'Paris' and one side was 'Academy In Peril' and they gave you a free poster by an artist evoking the texture of the record. Jesus, I took one look and thought, 'If that's what it means I'm gonna jump out of the window.' Grey block-slabs of concrete and no colour.
JOHN CALE, FEBRUARY 1983

John Cale – Substage in a hard hat.

FEAR

Fear is a man's best friend.
JOHN CALE, 1974

A catchy chunk of intellectualised paranoia.
ROBIN DENSELOW, *THE GUARDIAN*, NOVEMBER 1974

Island have signed me for six albums in three years. God knows how I'll do it. I'm concerned with a more simple approach to my writing – also orchestral arrangements. Nothing grand, but certainly something interesting. The songs are together and I'm going to talk to Phil Manzanera of Roxy about getting a band together for the sessions.
JOHN CALE, APRIL 1974

These songs really make me feel like I'm a songwriter for the first time.
JOHN CALE, OCTOBER 1974

ON THE ROAD

(Cale's) low-key entrance in June 1 ended with a haunted, necrophiliac airing of 'Heartbreak Hotel' that was transfixing, Cale rooted to one spot, sloughing energy like an erupting volcano. The next time he performed it he exploded, spinning across the stage into a chair, falling onto the floor then picking it up and running full tilt, chair at arm's length. At the Berlin Nico concert he performed 'Fear', smashing water-filled wine glasses lined up across the piano with a knife during the chorus. For his début solo tour in September 1974 (eventually cancelled) he had planned The Westminster Boys' Choir singing 'Surf's Up' and the lyrics of 'Guts' decorated by a half side of beef held by two lab coated assistants while Cale pointed anatomically, climaxing with a bucket of entrails which he would fling at the audience.
JOHN INGHAM, *LET IT ROCK*, AUGUST 1975

June 1 gave me more confidence than anything. I knew I could go out there and sing songs, but that isn't enough. You have to go out there and do something to the people. That was the beauty of this opportunity. I could go out there and – again negate the songs – you know, I really didn't have that much confidence in the songs. I haven't written any blockbusters, I haven't written a 'Heroin' yet. That's a classic, a catalyst, a real ball-breaker.
JOHN CALE, AUGUST 1975

I was getting lazy. I didn't have any confidence. I kept putting it off and putting it off. But I love performing. I don't like performing repetitive things, but I think I'll be better in the studio for being on the road.
JOHN CALE, MAY 1975

It's a great relief being able to talk to an audience. I figured in the beginning – it's very easy to go out there and set up a band and hide behind it. But when you get where you're yelling and people are yelling back, that's great.
JOHN CALE, AUGUST 1975

Touring with Cale was great fun and I enjoyed it a lot. When we started off that tour, it was insane, because we didn't know the songs, we didn't know the keys, we didn't know what the hell we were doing, so there were a lot of theatrics in the hope that the audience wouldn't spot what was going on.
CHRIS THOMAS, 1982

I want to do a song where you never know what the song is going to be. Pick two chords and if you don't have anything to say, don't say anything. Then you're at least working from a point of honesty so that people can see something grow if it grows from there. That's why I do 'Waiting For The Man'. It's much easier for me to turn into a dramatic situation than my own songs, because it's more open-ended. My songs have similar dramatic situations, but I congest my lyrics so much. 'Guts', for instance, could be made to work that way, but it can't with the amount of words that I have in it. 'Waiting For The Man' is very economical in terms of lyric, very precise.
JOHN CALE, AUGUST 1975

My lyrics . . . were getting more and more suicidal. I was testing myself, pushing to see how far I could go. 'Fear' had few concepts . . . arrangements in it. It doesn't expand.
JOHN CALE, NOVEMBER 1974

I didn't think I could carry a concert before. Now I think I can. Just listen to the new album.
JOHN CALE, APRIL 1974

John was going on stage as The Invisible Man, trailing bandages around everywhere, for us all to trip over.
DAVEY O'LIST, NOVEMBER 1982

ELVIS PRESLEY

I thought he died when I recorded 'Heartbreak Hotel'.
JOHN CALE, AUGUST 1977

SLOW DAZZLE

I want to see if I can write singles. The fact that people buy a record – it's like saying something to someone. If you like a record it shows that someone's saying something to you. I don't want to get philosophical about it but there's a human side to the charts.
JOHN CALE, MAY 1975

Love and all that shit isn't necessarily what rock is about. What it is is you pick up on the potential of a situation and expand it into something that hasn't been realised the way it is right now. If you push it far enough it'll develop into something else.
JOHN CALE, AUGUST 1975

Listen to 'Slow Dazzle'. He's trying to get into The Velvets thing, too. We talk about it all the time.
LOU REED, JANUARY 1976

'Slow Dazzle' sold best, but the others keep chugging along.
JOHN CALE, FEBRUARY 1983

'Guts' . . . would have stopped Rommel in his tracks if the British had had it in 1942.
ADAM SWEETING, *MELODY MAKER*, FEBRUARY 1984

HELEN OF TROY

The notion of placing trust in a personality as volatile and erratic as John Cale was, I admit, a daft one right from the beginning.
PETE ERSKINE, *NME*, DECEMBER 1975

Cale is having an even harder time than Uncle Lou in moving on from the albatross of The Velvet Underground . . . he's become a kind of chemical Neil Sedaka sitting up there at his Steinway dealing out medleys for well-dressed and well-spaced audiences to OD to.
CHRIS SALEWICZ, *NME*, NOVEMBER 1975

Patti Smith, New York street poetess harnessed by Cale on the seminal "Horses".

The trouble was, Island had their own idea of what that record should sound like. They wanted to include songs I didn't particularly like, but it was also an impertinent assumption on my part that I was capable of managing myself. My determination to have 'Helen Of Troy' come out the way it did was not really fair on Island or on my management, especially at a time when Island was losing its percentage of the market, which was making everybody very paranoid.
JOHN CALE, SEPTEMBER 1985

PATTI SMITH

John didn't produce 'Horses' really, we did. But he helped by being there.
PATTI SMITH, MARCH 1977

John's an artist and I don't wanna waste John's time trying to figure out what place to plug my microphone in. It's a waste of time for John to work with me.
PATTI SMITH, OCTOBER 1976

Production wise, with our record he wanted to put strings on it and new musicians. John loves The Beach Boys. If you're into some Velvet Underground fantasy, forget it. John is into The Beach Boys – totally. When he wanted me, he wanted to just get rid of the band and take me in with an orchestra. It's cool . . . I'll work with John again in 10 years. Me and John'll do a Ronettes record.
PATTI SMITH, OCTOBER 1976

Clockwise, from top left: Eno, Nico, John Cale and Kevin Ayers.

What Patti said about the group having produced 'Horses' is like . . . well, if I told you that isn't Patti singing on the album, it's me, you wouldn't believe me, would you?
JOHN CALE, SEPTEMBER 1977

We check each other out. We're very aware of each other, though she is a bit noisy. I kinda like her. She was mixing her last album at the Record Plant when I was recording mine in the next studio. One night she came to listen to what I'd been doing. She was very quiet for a change. When she'd heard a few tracks she just looked at me and said, 'How come an absolute bastard like you can make such beautiful music?'
LOU REED, JUNE 1977

Patti Smith was a poet who wanted to be a róck 'n' roll star, wanted to be Keith Richards or whatever. So with a band that had never been into a studio before you had to make them feel that they were really good musicians to allow room for Patti's poetry to come through, which is why we had the idea of improvising poetry against poetry.
JOHN CALE, FEBRUARY 1984

My last organ has been stolen from me a month ago and Patti Smith bought me this one here. I was down and out in Paris and I thought, 'Well, what was I going to do without my organ?' And then a friend of mine had just seen the same organ as the one I had before in a small place, the only one in Paris and Patti Smith bought it for me. Isn't that beautiful. She was very, very incredible. I said, 'I'll give you back the money very quickly, as soon as I have it', and she said, 'No, no, it's a present from me. I don't need any money now.'
NICO, JUNE 1978

I hope she comes back and gives Pet Banatar or Pat Benatar or whatever her name is a fright. I wish she'd come back and make another record. As a poet she wanted to be Keith Richards.
JOHN CALE, MAY 1985

ANIMAL JUSTICE

I cut a chicken's head off on-stage. A whole bunch of people walked off – they were all vegetarians. They wanted to know before it happened, 'What are you gonna do, are you going to hurt it?' I said no, and afterwards they told me I lied to them. I said, 'I didn't hurt it, I killed it. It didn't feel a thing.'
JOHN CALE, SEPTEMBER 1979

ILLEGAL PRODUCTIONS

No I'm not going to produce the Squeeze album. I'm growing sideburns.
JOHN CALE, 1977

John wanted us to call the album 'Gay Guys'. No way!
CHRIS DIFFORD, JULY 1978

Menace, who I'm producing, they're all about 2ft 6ins. dwarfs and they hang onto the mike stands singing lines like, 'I want nothing/Look at all the money Howard Hughes, J Paul Getty got/I'd be happier if I was covered in soot.'
JOHN CALE, SEPTEMBER 1977

SPY *VS* SPY

Spy has been a toy of mine for a long time. I was really happy when we first put it together, but then we had a disagreement with our backer. We've been trying to put the whole thing back together for about a year.
JOHN CALE, SEPTEMBER 1979

We've got a single out by Lester Bangs and an EP by the Model Citizens. I'm trying to get this tape of a four-tune jam I did with Mick Ronson, Ian Hunter, and Corky Laing. I don't know if it's going to work out – there's going to be a lot of legal baloney to sort out.
JOHN CALE, SEPTEMBER 1979

We were up all night, playing old rock 'n' roll numbers. John was around, playing on Ian's latest album, and this all night jam just developed in the studio.
MICK RONSON, SEPTEMBER 1984

That was when New York was burgeoning with rock 'n' roll bands. Harry Toledo And The Rockets . . . they became The Necessaries, then Chris Spedding joined them and they fell apart.
JOHN CALE, FEBRUARY 1984

Spy's sort of moribund. There was a sort of disagreement between my partner (manager Jane Friedman) and I, we split up and . . . you know the usual mess that was going on.
JOHN CALE, FEBRUARY 1984

READY FOR WAR

I should have said, 'We have an induction room backstage. Let's see you come back and enlist.' But I have received a lot of reactions during this tour. Even some of the guys who devise war games at the Pentagon have come to the shows. It looks like I've finally made an American album.
JOHN CALE, AUGUST 1980

I bet they're ready – like hell.
JOHN CALE, AUGUST 1980

Right now America has this lingering 'weak-sister' image, but that's because both America and Russia attempt to make deals about the rest of the world while working under the threat of nuclear confrontation. That renders it impossible to conduct meaningful foreign policy; you can never decisively determine anything.
JOHN CALE, AUGUST 1980

I think it's important for people to go through the nuclear barrier. You've got to experience a nuclear war and find out exactly what it does, how people live in the face of it and after the fact of it. And that is going to happen. There's no reason, though, to force those notions on people. I suspect that Marianne Faithful and Warren Zevon are more effective at putting across some of the things I'm interested in; their ways are at least more digestible. I'm afraid nobody really wants to hear what I'm singing about.
JOHN CALE, AUGUST 1980

If I wanted to be prophetic I'd be quite happy doing 'Please Crawl Out Of Your Window'. Fuck 'Ready For War'. All the people in the audience are yelling and stamping their feet and saying, 'Yeah, right on!' If I stopped the band playing and said, 'Okay, all you guys that are singing along, line up at the back for induction . . . ' You wouldn't see one of them. If you stole a hubcap off one of them, though, you'd probably hear from him.
JOHN CALE, APRIL 1981

Military Intelligence isn't what it used to be – so what? Human intelligence isn't what it used to be either.
JOHN CALE, 'SABOTAGE', 1979

HONI SOIT

I gather from what you're telling me that if I'm not careful I might actually become successful.
JOHN CALE, APRIL 1981

Just for the sake of argument, can you imagine if my album ever went Top 10? All of a sudden there would be a hell of a lot of backbiting, 'Ah, Cale goes commercial.' Even without my going commercial. I'd have no sense of identity if I did that. I'm very insecure about that. I use cracks on the sidewalk to walk down the street. I'd always walk on the lines. I never take anything but a calculated risk, and I do it because it gives me a sense of identity.
JOHN CALE, APRIL 1981

I used a producer on this album because I couldn't have done it without one. I went in there and told Mike (Thorne), 'Look, I've got a problem. Before I go into a studio I rehearse all the shit until it turns into vapour. But by the time I get into the studio I'm so bored with that shit that what's going to happen is I'm going to start making up songs and one thing will lead to another. I need a record of what I'm going to do in there.' So I had cassettes of the first six days, tape machines running continuously. And we ended up with three times as much material as we intended to do.
JOHN CALE, APRIL 1981

MUSIC FOR A NEW SOCIETY

I wanted to do a 'Marble Index' – you take my songs, put the songs down, then write independent arrangements around them. It's an arranger's record. The whole thing is based on arrangements. There are melodies there, but some of it even goes outside the realm of that, it's like the BBC Radiophonic Workshop.
JOHN CALE, FEBRUARY 1983

It was intended to be a proper solo album, which was something that I'd never done. Initially the idea was to stick me in a studio with a piano and have me just play the songs like that. There was a purist notion of what it was supposed to be, but it flowered into something entirely different, with a lot of overdubbings. The only one with a band on the whole album is 'Changes Made' and that shouldn't be there, but the record company insisted on it.
JOHN CALE, FEBRUARY 1983

John Cale – would you buy a used Lou Reed picture from this man?

What I was most interested in was the terror of the moment.
JOHN CALE, FEBRUARY 1983

Oh, it's a bleak one all right, but it wasn't made to make people jump out of windows. They wouldn't jump out of windows anyway – they wouldn't buy the damned album.
JOHN CALE, FEBRUARY 1983

The whole thing is hooked on the voice, which is one thing I'm really proud of, that the voice is sticking out there, that it's not hidden.
JOHN CALE, FEBRUARY 1983

It was improvised, but it was romantic. Freudian. 'Tortuous' is a good word for it.
JOHN CALE, FEBRUARY 1984

There were some examples where songs ended up so emaciated they weren't songs any more.
JOHN CALE, FEBRUARY 1984

'Music For A New Society' was my best received record ever and it bombed. And I wanna sell records. I don't want eulogies. I'll leave them for my gravestone. John Cale – Va Va Voom.
JOHN CALE, SEPTEMBER 1985

John Cale, all blacked up and nowhere to go.

CARIBBEAN SUNSET

The songs on 'Caribbean Sunset' are pretty tight and they don't pretend to be . . . 'Model Beirut Recital' is sort of idiosyncratic. It sort of lurches along well-intentionally . . . the worst thing about the album is that some of the songs might be cute.
JOHN CALE, FEBRUARY 1984

That guy at the beginning of 'Model Beirut Recital', the Palestinian, says 'Beirut you're a whore and you've been raped. I spit on you . . . ' And the rest of it is just Israeli back-chatter. It was a pretty considered way to deal with an obnoxious subject in a passionate, sympathetic way.
JOHN CALE, MARCH 1984

ARTIFICIAL INTELLIGENCE

We had three and a half weeks to complete it. Ridiculous. We spent one week writing material and then we went in and threw half of it out. All the records were done like that. Give me five grand and you can have the cassettes.
JOHN CALE, OCTOBER 1985

I am a ham. I've no business being in rock 'n' roll. I've said over and over again that I'm a classical composer, dishevelling my musical personality by dabbling in rock 'n' roll.
JOHN CALE, OCTOBER 1985

Some of 'Artificial Intelligence' will do for the moment, but not much of it.
ALLAN JONES, *MELODY MAKER*, AUGUST 1985

I'm very pleased with 'Artificial Intelligence' because, for a change, there's more singing in there than screaming.
JOHN CALE, SEPTEMBER 1985

Some of it is psychotic. It has that element, but it's down-played and it's more effective that way. Just sing the song, don't get excited, just take a little blue pill. But I don't fancy being remembered as the author of a series of records which were put out as rock 'n' roll records when, in fact, they had nothing to do with rock 'n' roll. I am not a rock 'n' roll musician.
JOHN CALE, SEPTEMBER 1985

FALLEN KNIGHTS AND FALLEN LADIES

And if it's true, all so true, that you can't live up to everyone's expectations, and if it's true you cannot be all things to all people, and if it's true you cannot be other than what you are (passage of time to the contrary), then you must be strong of heart if you wish to work the problem out in public, on stage, through work before 'them' who fully expect and predict in print their idol's fall. And if it was true it was inevitable and oh yes, we know sad, and oh nothing could be done about it after all. That's how she started out. She just realised too late the habits of years are not undone in days, then if it's true that princesses are besmirched, then all of us are fallen knights.
LOU REED, *FALLEN KNIGHTS AND FALLEN LADIES*, 1974

That's a good, pretentiously aggressive ending!
LOU REED, DECEMBER 1976

NICO (1940?-1988)

Nico was unique. She styled herself, or at least, allowed herself to be styled, an enigma; she had nothing to do with rock 'n' roll, but exerted a fascination few rock 'n' rollers could ever aspire to.

Discovered by Andrew Loog Oldham, brought to fame by Andy Warhol, a companion of Brian Jones, Bob Dylan, Leonard Cohen, Jim Morrison and Iggy Pop, by the early 1970s she was already a legend, and one who attracted the attention of all who came within her orbit. Brian Eno and Kevin Ayers, anarchic genii in their own right, recorded with her, David Bowie professed an interest and, according to Nico herself, spent several years fruitlessly pursuing her.

Later in the decade, without a contract, she was brought back to the stage by The Pop Group's manager, and given support slots alongside the likes of The Adverts and The Banshees, unhappy performances marred by an audience lulled into the belief that all The Velvet Underground stood for was chaos and energy. When John Cooper Clarke, standing in for DJ Nicky Horne on Capital Radio, played 'Janitor Of Lunacy', Horne was furious.

Nico in the Eighties *was* accepted. Courted by the fresh young things erupting out of the Manchester scene, aided by the neo-rock sensibilities of 'Drama Of Exile', and finally finding a contemporary audience via the bats and belfries of the emergent Gothic scene, she toured regularly, recorded sporadically, and acolytes of her earliest records became almost accustomed to hearing her.

But even familiarity could not dull her mystique, not even the harsh electric light of her latter-day visibility could sweep away all the flickering grotesqueries of her gaslight intricacies.

Nico's music was as timeless as she, herself, appeared to be. Her birth date – different sources quote different dates, anywhere between 1938-1943, her birthplace – Budapest? Cologne? – were secrets she guarded fiercely. She could, with her beauty and mystery, have been another Marianne Faithful; when Andrew Oldham presented her to the world on his nascent Immediate label in 1965, possibly that is what he intended. But the world to which she was exposed, and the private world which existed within her, would not tolerate such an easy option. When she recorded her first solo album, her record company tried to sweeten the brew with syrup and strings. Nico shone through regardless.

Later, in tandem with John Cale, she recorded not one, not two, but three of the most important records of the early seventies, and caught in isolation – her majestic rendering of 'The End' on 'June 1 1974', the icy blast of 'Lawns Of Dawn' on a misguided Elektra sampler in 1971 – the shafts of light which filtered through the darkened splendour of her musical cathedrals put matters in a perspective which a simple pop record should never be capable of.

A heart attack in the sun whilst bicycling in Spain, Nico did not die the death most people expected. There again, she didn't live the life most people expected either.

DISCOGRAPHY

ORIGINAL RELEASES ONLY – COMPILATIONS LISTED ONLY WHEN UNRELEASED MATERIAL IS INCLUDED.

VELVET UNDERGROUND ORIGINAL RECORDINGS (USA)

8/66: **THE EAST VILLAGE OTHER ELECTRIC NEWSPAPER** (LP)
including 'Noise' (ESP 1034)

12/66: **LOOP** (FLEXIDISC) Free with *Aspen* magazine

2/67: **CONVERSATION** (FLEXIDISC) Free with Andy Warhol's *Index Book*

VELVET UNDERGROUND SINGLES (USA)

3/67: **ALL TOMORROW'S PARTIES/I'LL BE YOUR MIRROR**
(VERVE 10466)

6/67: **SUNDAY MORNING/FEMME FATALE**
(VERVE PROMO)

2/68: **WHITE LIGHT WHITE HEAT/HERE SHE COMES NOW**
(VERVE PROMO)

3/68: **I HEARD HER CALL MY NAME/HERE SHE COMES NOW**
(VERVE 10560)

3/69: **JESUS/WHAT GOES ON**
(MGM K14057)

9/70: **WHO LOVES THE SUN/SWEET JANE**
(COTILLION 44107)

VELVET UNDERGROUND SINGLES (UK)

4/71: **WHO LOVES THE SUN/SWEET JANE**
(ATLANTIC 2091 088)

6/76: **WHITE HEAT** (EP):
'I'm Sticking With You'/'Ferryboat Bill'/'Inside Your Heart'/
'Foggy Notion'
(AEB 301)

VELVET UNDERGROUND LPs (UK)

10/67: **THE VELVET UNDERGROUND AND NICO** (LP)
(VERVE SVLP 9184 – US RELEASE 3/67)
NB: 1988 CD release features unreleased version of 'All Tomorrow's
Parties' (Verve 8232902)

5/68: **WHITE LIGHT WHITE HEAT**
(VERVE SVLP 9201 – US RELEASE 3/68)

5/69: **THE VELVET UNDERGROUND**
(MGM CS 8108 – US RELEASE 3/69)

4/71: **LOADED**
(ATLANTIC 2400 111 – US RELEASE 9/70)

8/72: **LIVE AT MAX'S KANSAS CITY**
(ATLANTIC K30022 – US RELEASE 5/72)
NB: Billy Yule deputises for Maureen Tucker on above LP, recorded the
day before Lou left the band.

2/73: **SQUEEZE THE VELVET UNDERGROUND**
(POLYDOR 2383 180)
NB: Above LP features Morrison alone of earlier Velvets incarnations.
Other members included Willie 'Boom Boom' Alexander and Doug and
Billy Yule.

/76: **EVIL MOTHERS**
(SKYDOG 003 – FRANCE)
NB: Above LP includes three tracks recorded at Max's, shortly before
the show which produced 'Live At Max's'.

3/79: **LIVE 1969**
(MERCURY 6643 900). Originally available as US import, 1974.

/80: **ETCETERA**
(PLASTIC INEVITABLE RECORDS FIRST 1)*

/82: **AND SO ON**
(PLASTIC INEVITABLE RECORDS SECOND 1)*

/84: **EVERYTHING YOU WANTED TO KNOW ABOUT . . .**
(PLASTIC INEVITABLE RECORDS)*

2/85: **VU**
(POLYDOR POLD 5167) *

/88: **ANOTHER VIEW**
(POLYDOR 8294051) *

* Compilation includes previously unreleased/archive material

JOHN CALE DISCOGRAPHY

WITH THE PRIMITIVES
SNEAKY PETE/THE OSTRICH
See under Lou Reed

WITH LAMONTE YOUNG'S THEATRE OF ETERNAL MUSIC

/64: **LAMONTE YOUNG'S DREAM SYNDICATE** (LP)

WITH THE VELVET UNDERGROUND
All releases up to and including 'White Light White Heat'

WITH TERRY RILEY

4/71: **THE CHURCH OF ANTHRAX** (LP)

JOHN CALE SINGLES (UK)

7/70: **FAIRWEATHER FRIEND/CLEO**
(COLUMBIA PROMO – US)

9/70: **HELLO THERE/GIDEON'S BIBLE**
(COLUMBIA PROMO – US)

12/70: **BIG WHITE CROWD/GHOST STORY**
(COLUMBIA PROMO – US)

8/72: **DAYS OF STEAM/LEGS LARRY AT THE TELEVISION CENTRE**
(REPRISE PROMO – US)

10/74: **THE MAN WHO COULDN'T AFFORD TO/SYLVIA SAID**
(ISLAND WIP 6202)

8/77: **ANIMAL JUSTICE** (EP):
'Chicken Shit'/'Memphis'/'Hedda Gabbler'
(ILLEGAL IL 003)

JACK THE RIPPER IN THE MOULIN ROUGE/MEMPHIS
(ILLEGAL IL 006 – UNRELEASED)

1/80: **MERCENARIES/ROSE GARDEN FUNERAL OF SORES**
(SPY 001 – US)

5/81: **DEAD OR ALIVE/HONI SOIT**
(A&M AMS 8130)

3/83: **CLOSE WATCH/CLOSE WATCH**
(ZE WIP)
NB: A-side taken from 'Music For A New Society' LP, B-side from LP
'Helen Of Troy'.

9/84: **OOH LA LA/NEVER GONNA GIVE YOU UP**
(ZE WIP)

7/85: **DYING ON THE VINE/EVERY TIME THE DOGS BARK**
(BEGGARS BANQUET BEG 145)

11/85: **SATELLITE WALK/DYING ON THE VINE**
(BEGGARS BANQUET BEG 153)

11/85: **SATELLITE WALK/DYING ON THE VINE/CRASH COURSE IN HARMONICS**
(BEGGARS BANQUET BEG 153T)

JOHN CALE LPs

7/70: **VINTAGE VIOLENCE**
(COLUMBIA CS 1037 – US)

7/72: **THE ACADEMY IN PERIL**
(REPRISE REP 44212 – US)

3/73: **PARIS 1919**
(REPRISE K44239)

9/74: **FEAR**
(ISLAND ILPS 9301)

4/75: **SLOW DAZZLE**
(ISLAND ILPS 9317)

11/75: **HELEN OF TROY**
(ISLAND ILPS 9350)
NB: Two versions of the above LP were released. Original pressings
included 'Leaving It Up To You'. Later copies replaced this with
'Coral Moon'.

2/77: **GUTS**
(ISLAND ILPS 9459) *

* Compilation includes previously unreleased material.

12/79: **SABOTAGE – LIVE**
(SPY SP 004 – US)

3/81: **HONI SOIT**
(A&M AMLH 64948)

7/83: **MUSIC FOR A NEW SOCIETY**
(ZE ILPS 7019)

1/84: **CARIBBEAN SUNSET**
(ZE ILPS 7024)

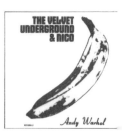

THE VELVET UNDERGROUND AND NICO

WHITE LIGHT WHITE HEAT

RIS 1919

OW DAZZLE

9/84:   **JOHN CALE COMES ALIVE**
(ZE ILPS 7026)

10/85:   **ARTIFICIAL INTELLIGENCE**
(BEGGARS BANQUET BEGA 68)

JOHN CALE/NICO/ENO/KEVIN AYERS DISCOGRAPHY

7/74:   **JUNE 1 1974**
(ISLAND ILPS 9291)

WITH NICO

CHELSEA GIRL (LP)

THE MARBLE INDEX (LP)

DESERT SHORE (LP)

THE END (LP)

CAMERA OBSCURA (LP)

See under Nico for details

JOHN CALE SESSION APPEARANCES

(Sessions marked * denote Joe Boyd productions, Cale being
a regular Boyd sideman 1970-77.)

WITH MORNING GLORY

/68:   **TWO SUNS WORTH** (LP – engineer)
(FONTANA SRF 67573)

WITH EARTH OPERA

/69:   **GREAT AMERICAN EAGLE TRAGEDY** (LP)
(ELEKTRA EKS 4038)

WITH THE STOOGES

/69:   **THE STOOGES** (LP – producer)
(ELEKTRA 42055)

/69:   **I WANNA BE YOUR DOG/1969** (45 – producer)
(ELEKTRA 45664 – US)

WITH TAX FREE

/70:   **TAX FREE**
(POLYDOR 244053)

WITH NICK DRAKE*

/70:   **BRYTER LAYTER** (LP)
(ISLAND ILPS 9134)

WITH MIKE HERON*

/71:   **SMILING MEN WITH BAD REPUTATIONS**
(ISLAND ILPS 9146)
NB: One track on above LP, 'Warm Heart Pastry', links Cale and Heron
with Pete Townshend, Keith Moon and John Entwistle under the name
Tommy And The Bijoux.

/71:   **CALL ME DIAMOND/LADY WONDER** (45)
(ISLAND WIP 6101)

WITH JENNIFER WARNES

/72:   **JENNIFER** (LP – producer)
(REPRISE MS 2065)
NB: Above LP includes one otherwise unavailable Cale song, 'Empty
Bottles', performed by Cale at the 1972 Paris Bataclan gig with Nico
and Lou Reed.

WITH CHUNKY, NOVA AND ERNIE

/73:   **CHUNKY, NOVA AND ERNIE** (LP – producer)
(REPRISE MS 2146)

WITH SILVERHEAD

/73:   **SIXTEEN AND SAVAGED** (LP – producer)
(PURPLE TPSA 7511)

WITH GEOFF MULDAUR*

10/75:   **HAVING A WONDERFUL TIME** (LP)
(REPRISE K54046)

WITH ENO

/75:   **ANOTHER GREEN WORLD** (LP)
(ISLAND ILPS 9051)

/78:   **MUSIC FOR FILMS** (LP)
(EG EGED 5)

WITH PATTI SMITH

6/76:   **GLORIA/MY GENERATION** (45)
(ARISTA 136)

6/76:   **HORSES** (LP – producer)
(ARISTA ARTY 122)

WITH MODERN LOVERS

/76:   **MODERN LOVERS** (LP – producer)
(BESERKLEY BSERK 1)

7/77:   **ROADRUNNER TWICE** (45 – producer)
(BESERKLEY BZZ 1)

WITH KATE AND ANNA McGARRIGLE*

2/77:   **DANCER WITH BRUISED KNEES** (LP)
(WB K56356)

WITH JULIE COVINGTON*

10/77:   **ONLY WOMEN BLEED/EASY TO SLIP** (45)
(VIRGIN VS 196)

12/77:   **JULIE COVINGTON** (LP)
(VIRGIN V2107)

WITH SHAM 69

7/77:   **I DON'T WANNA/ULSTER/RED LONDON** (45 – producer)
(STEP FORWARD SF 4)

WITH MENACE

7/77:   **SCREWED UP** (EP – producer)
(ILLEGAL IL 004)

WITH SQUEEZE

7/77:   **PACKET OF THREE** (45 – producer)
(DFC 001)

3/78:   **SQUEEZE** (LP – producer)
(A&M AMLH 68465)

/78:   **WRONG WAY** (flexidisc – producer)
(*SMASH HITS*, FREEBIE)

WITH HARRY TOLEDO

/78:   **HARRY TOLEDO AND THE ROCKETS** (EP – producer)
(SPY 001)

WITH DAVID KUBINEC

12/78:   **SOME THINGS NEVER CHANGE** (LP – producer)
(A&M AMLH 68501)

WITH DAVID BOWIE

10/78:   **PIANO-LA/VELVET COUCH** (unissued)

WITH MARIE ET LES GARCONS

/79:   **ATTITUDE/REBOP** (45 – producer)
(ZE 7002)

WITH IAN HUNTER

/79:   **YOU'RE NEVER ALONE WITH A SCHIZOPHRENIC**
(CHRYSALIS 1214)

WITH THE NECESSARIES

10/79:   **YOU CAN BORROW MY CAR/RUNAWAY CHILD** (45 – producer)
(SPY 002)

WITH DORIAN

4/80:   **MODERN GUY** (LP – producer)
(CEL 2-6546)

4/80:   **UNE NOUVELLE VIE** (French language version of above)
(DIS 217)

WITH GENE LOVES JEZEBEL

10/84:   sessions; unissued

STERLING MORRISON DISCOGRAPHY

WITH THE VELVET UNDERGROUND

All LPs/singles

NICO DISCOGRAPHY

WITH THE VELVET UNDERGROUND

THE VELVET UNDERGROUND AND NICO LP and accompanying singles

NICO SINGLES (UK)

8/65:   **I'M NOT SAYING/THE LAST MILE**
(IMMEDIATE IM 003)

9/81:   **VEGAS/SAETA**
(FLICKNIFE FLS 206)

2/82:   **I'M NOT SAYING/THE LAST MILE**
(IMMEDIATE IM 003)

7/82:   **PROCESSION/ALL TOMORROW'S PARTIES**
(HALF RECORDS REC 1)

7/82:   **PROCESSION/ALL TOMORROW'S PARTIES/SECRET SIDE/
FEMME FATALE**
(HALF RECORDS REC 1)

6/83:   **HEROES/ONE MORE CHANCE**
(AURA AUS 137)

6/85:   **MY FUNNY VALENTINE/MY HEART IS EMPTY**
(BEGGARS BANQUET BEG 139/139T)

10/85:   **I'M WAITING FOR THE MAN/PURPLE LIPS**
(AURA AUS 147)

NICO LPs (UK)

7/69:   **THE MARBLE INDEX**
(MGM EKL/EKS 74029)

1/71:   **DESERT SHORE**
(REPRISE RSLP 6424)

10/71:   **CHELSEA GIRL**
(VERVE MGM 2353 025 – US RELEASE 10/67)

10/74:   **THE END**
(ISLAND ILPS 9311)

7/81:   **DRAMA OF EXILE**
(AURA AUL 715)

/83:   **DO OR DIE**
(ROIR A117)

LSEA GIRL

7/85:   **CAMERA OBSCURA**
        (BEGGARS BANQUET BEAG 63)

8/85:   **THE BLUE ANGEL**
        (AURA AUL 731)*

        * Compilation includes unreleased material

4/86:   **BEHIND THE IRON CURTAIN**
        (CASTLE COMMUNICATIONS DOJOLP 27)

/87:   **LIVE IN TOKYO**
        (CASTLE COMMUNICATIONS DOJOLP 50)
        WITH JOHN CALE/ENO/KEVIN AYERS
        LP 'June 1 1974' – see John Cale for details.

NICO SESSION APPEARANCES
WITH KEVIN AYERS
8/74:   **THE CONFESSIONS OF DR DREAM** (LP)
        (ISLAND ILPS 9263)

WITH BAUHAUS
10/82: **WAITING FOR THE MAN** (45)
        (BEGGARS BANQUET BEG 83T)

        NB: 'My Eyes Have Seen You', on The Doors' 'Strange Days'
        (Elektra 74014), 'Decadence' on Kevin Ayers' 'Bananamour'
        (HARVEST SHVL 807) and 'Joan Of Arc' on Leonard Cohen's 'Songs Of
        Love And Hate' (CBS 69004) were all apparently written about/for Nico.

LOU REED DISCOGRAPHY
WITH THE SHADES
/62:   **SO BLUE/LEAVE HER FOR ME**
        (TIME 1002)

WITH THE BEACHNUTS
/65:   **CYCLE ANNIE***

WITH THE ROUGHNECKS
/65:   **YOU'RE DRIVING ME INSANE ***

        * Both included on LP 'Soundsville'
        (DLP 187)

WITH THE PRIMITIVES
/65:   **THE OSTRICH/SNEAKY PETE**
        (PICKWICK CITY 001)

WITH THE VELVET UNDERGROUND
All original releases up to and including 'Max's Kansas City'

LOU REED SOLO SINGLES (UK)
3/72:   **WALK IT AND TALK IT/WILD CHILD**
        (RCA 2240)

5/73:   **WALK ON THE WILD SIDE/PERFECT DAY**
        (RCA 2303)

8/73:   **VICIOUS/SATELLITE OF LOVE**
        (RCA 2318)

10/73: **SATELLITE OF LOVE/VICIOUS**
        (RCA 2318)

2/74:   **CAROLINE SAYS I/CAROLINE SAYS II**
        (RCA APBO 0221)

5/74:   **SWEET JANE/LADY DAY**
        (RCA APBO 0238)

10/74: **SALLY CAN'T DANCE/ENNUI**
        (RCA 2467)

12/75: **CHARLEY'S GIRL/NOWHERE AT ALL**
        (RCA 2666)

2/76:   **CRAZY FEELING/NOWHERE AT ALL**
        (RCA 10648)

10/76: **ROCK 'N' ROLL HEART/SENSELESSLY CRUEL**
        (ARISTA 105)

4/77:   **WALK ON THE WILD SIDE/PERFECT DAY**
        (RCA 2303)

2/78:   **STREET HASSLE/WAITING FOR THE MAN/VENUS IN FURS**
        (ARISTA 12198)

5/79:   **CITY LIGHTS/DISCO MYSTIC**
        (ARISTA 308)

8/81:   **WALK ON THE WILD SIDE/VICIOUS**
        (Old Gold 523)

12/83: **BLUE MASK/WALK ON THE WILD SIDE**
        (RCA PC 9352)

5/84:   **I LOVE YOU SUZANNE/VICIOUS**
        (RCA 417)

LOU REED ALBUMS (UK)
6/72:   **LOU REED**
        (RCA LSP 4701)

11/72: **TRANSFORMER**
        (RCA LSP 4807)

9/73:   **BERLIN**
        (RCA RS 1002)

3/74:   **ROCK 'N' ROLL ANIMAL**
        (RCA APLI 0472)

10/74: **SALLY CAN'T DANCE**
        (RCA APLI 06011)

3/75:   **LOU REED LIVE**
        (RCA RS 1007)

7/75:   **METAL MACHINE MUSIC**
        (RCA CPL-2 1101) US only

12/75: **CONEY ISLAND BABY**
        (RCA RS 1035)

11/76: **ROCK AND ROLL HEART**
        (ARISTA ARTY 142)

3/78:   **STREET HASSLE**
        (ARISTA SPART 1045)

3/79:   **TAKE NO PRISONERS**
        (RCA XL 03066-2)

5/79:   **THE BELLS**
        (ARISTA SPART 1093)

5/80:   **GROWING UP IN PUBLIC**
        (ARISTA SPART 1131)

3/82:   **THE BLUE MASK**
        (RCA LP 6028)

3/83:   **LEGENDARY HEARTS**
        (RCA LP 6071)

4/84:   **NEW SENSATIONS**
        (RCA PL84998)

4/86:   **MISTRIAL**
        (RCA PL87190)

1/89:   **NEW YORK**
        (WEA WX246)

LOU REED SESSION APPEARANCES
WITH NICO
CHELSEA GIRLS
(see under Nico for details)

WITH NELSON SLATER
/76:   **WILD ANGELS** (LP – producer)
        (RCA APLI 1306 – US)

WITH GENYA RAVEN
/78:   **URBAN DESIRE**
        (20th Century BTH 8007)

        NB: Lou sings duet on one track, 'Aye Co'Lorado'. Genya also covers
        Cale's 'Darling I Need You' on this LP.

WITH KISS
11/81: **(MUSIC FROM) THE ELDER** (LP – lyricist)
        (Casablanca 6302 163)

11/81: **WORLD WITHOUT HEROES/MR BLACKWELL** (45 – lyricist)
        (Casablanca 2343)

        NB: 'Queen Bitch' on David Bowie's 'Hunky Dory'
        (RCA SF8244) was dedicated to Lou Reed: 'Some white heat returned
        with thanks.'

MAUREEN TUCKER DISCOGRAPHY
WITH THE VELVET UNDERGROUND
All releases up to and including 'Loaded'.

MAUREEN TUCKER SINGLE
/82:   **BE MY BABY/I'M STICKING WITH YOU**

WITH JONATHAN RICHMAN
(Count Joe Viglione's Vauvalen Records)

MAUREEN TUCKER LP
9/82:   **PLAYING POSSUM** (LP)
        (Trash Records)

BILLY YULE DISCOGRAPHY
WITH THE VELVET UNDERGROUND
LPs 'Live At Max's' and 'Squeeze'

DOUG YULE DISCOGRAPHY
WITH THE VELVET UNDERGROUND
All LPs and attendant singles post 'White Light White Heat'

WITH ELLIOTT MURPHY
/76:   **NIGHT LIGHTS**
        (RCA APLI 1318 – US ONLY)

WITH AMERICAN FLYER
/76:   **AMERICAN FLYER**
        (UA UAS 29991)

/77:   **SPIRIT OF WOMAN**
        (UA UAS 30078)

        NB: Yule later joined Lou Reed's live band for his 1975 tour.

ROCK 'N' ROLL ANIMAL

STREET HASSLE/WAITING FOR THE MAN/
VENUS IN FURS

TRANSFORMER

BERLIN